AF333165

THE BIBLE

THE BIBLE

WHERE DO YOU FIND IT AND WHAT DOES IT SAY?

RONALD H. ISAACS

JASON ARONSON INC.
Northvale, New Jersey
Jerusalem

This book was set in 11 pt. ITC Galliard by Alabama Book Composition of Deatsville, AL and printed and bound by Book-mart Press, Inc. of North Bergen, NJ.

10 9 8 7 6 5 4 3 2

Library of Congress Cataloging-in-Publication Data

Isaacs, Ronald H.
    The Bible : where do you find it, and what does it say? / Ronald H. Isaacs.
      p.   cm.
    Includes bibliographical references and index.
    ISBN 0-7657-6081-9
    1. Bible. O.T.—Criticism, interpretation, etc. 2. Judaism—Customs and Practices.
  I. Title.
BS1187.I83   2000   99-047830

Printed in the United States of America on acid-free paper. For information and catalog write to Jason Aronson Inc., 230 Livingston Street, Northvale, NJ 07647-1726, or visit our website: www.aronson.com

*For Rachel—
a very special mother-in-law*

Contents

Contents

Contents

Introduction

The Bible is the oldest and most widely read book in our civilization. It has been in continuous circulation for almost two thousand years and has been the source of religious ideals and values for millions of people. Ever since Sinai, the moral imperatives of the Five Books of Moses and the books of the Prophets have provided great inspiration to social reforms and religious idealists.

Throughout the English-speaking world many famous poets, dramatists, and novelists have studied the Bible for its profound ideas. Political ideas and institutions of American life have been shaped by biblical teachings.

Of course, it is in the realm of religion that the Bible is surely of paramount importance. As the holy book of both Judaism and Christianity, its influence has been momentous within the whole ethical framework of Western Civilization.

The many original biblical concepts whose ideas laid the foundation for Jewish civilization are scattered throughout the Bible. Because they are not arranged systematically, readers often have difficulty locating a particular idea of interest. Thus, the aim of this book is to systematize many of these concepts, arranging them in a way that will be easy to follow and to access.

A variety of concepts will be presented. Each concept will include the following:

Source: its biblical source (exact location in the Bible).

Details: further commentary that will help to amplify the concept and put it into its historical perspective.

In a Nutshell: a succinct summation of the rabbinic interpretation of the concept and how it is to be understood today.

Also included in the book is a listing of the weekly Bible portions and a brief summary of their contents. In addition, there is a listing of the most notable quotations that appear in each Bible portion.

There are eighty-three entries in this book, listed alphabetically for quick and easy access.

I hope that this book will help you appreciate the magnificent contribution the Bible has made to the people of the world. Perhaps, too, it will stimulate a more in-depth study of the Bible, one of the all-time best-selling books.

1
THE ADULTEROUS WIFE

If a man's wife has gone astray and broken faith with him . . . then he shall bring her to the priest.

—Numbers 5:11–31

DETAILS

The commandment of the adulterous wife (described in detail in Numbers 5:11–31) deals with the law of the suspicious husband who believes that his wife has been unfaithful to him. The suspicions of a jealous husband are proved or disproved by giving his wife "bitter water" and waiting to see the results of this ministration.

Many ordeals of jealously were known in the ancient Near East, including a parallel in the Babylonian Code of Hammurabi, where the river itself acts as the divine judge. In this commandment, the Bible gives the male partner clear prerogative by laying the burden of proof of innocence on the woman.

This commandment clearly implies that fidelity is an essential element in marriage and that jealousy is a legitimate sentiment, for trust is the foundation of the marital covenant.

THE ADULTEROUS WIFE IN A NUTSHELL

Nachmonides, in his explanation of the suspected adulterous wife, notes the Talmudic injunction that states that one should never rely on the occurrence of miracles. The exception, he states, involves the only biblical instance where a commandment is depended upon a miracle for its effectiveness. This was purposely designed by God, he says, so that a Jewish wife would never afford herself an opportunity to bear illegitimate children.

2

ANNUAL PILGRIMAGES TO JERUSALEM

Three times a year shall all your males appear before God in the place which He shall choose: on the feast of unleavened bread, and on the feast of weeks, and on the feast of tabernacles. And they shall not appear before God empty. Every man shall give as he is able, according to the blessings of the Lord your God which God has given you.

—Deuteronomy 16:13–17

DETAILS

Passover, Shavuot, and Sukkot are known as the three annual pilgrim festivals because of the three pilgrimages that adult Israelites had to make to the Sanctuary. Every adult Jew was required to make a pilgrimage to the Temple in Jerusalem on these three festivals and to bring with him the necessary animals for the various sacrifices. The three pilgrim festivals marked the spring (barley), summer (wheat), and autumn (fruit) harvests, respectively.

ANNUAL PILGRIMAGES TO JERUSALEM IN A NUTSHELL

According to the commentator Ibn Ezra, the three pilgrim festivals are called *shalosh regalim* because most of the pilgrims went to Jerusalem on foot. The traditional rule was that every pilgrim had to go on foot at least the final stage of the journey from the city of Jerusalem to the Temple Mount, since the expression *shalosh regalim* conveys the sense of three times on foot (Talmud *Chagigah* 1:1).

The commentator known as the Hinuch states the purpose of the pilgrimages was so the Jew could say thank-you to God for the miracles that God had performed on each of the three festivals. Although one could feel grateful at home, the special aura of a sanctuary would add to the sanctity and specialness of the occasion.

Today, the three festivals of Passover, Shavuot, and Sukkot are celebrated with much joy and enthusiasm. However, since the Jerusalem Temple no longer exists, there is no longer a need to bring sacrifices. Praying in the synagogue is the modern-day substitute for sacrifices.

3
BAKING *HALLAH*

When you eat of the bread of the land, you shall set apart
a portion for a gift unto God. Of the first of your dough you
shall set apart a cake for a gift; as that which is set apart
of the threshing floor, so shall you set it apart. Of the first of
your dough you shall give to the Lord a portion for a gift
throughout your generation.

—Numbers 15:19–21

DETAILS

The priest's share of the cake (*hallah*) donated in Temple times
to the *kohanim* is based on the biblical source quoted above
from the Book of Numbers, chapter 15. This law does not specify
what proportion of the dough should go to the priest. Thus the
talmudic rabbis defined *hallah* as one twenty-fourth of the loaf and
one forty-eighth from a baker.

BAKING *HALLAH* IN A NUTSHELL

The *hallah* offering is taken from wheat, barley, spelt, oats, and rye used in the baking of bread. If the *hallah* is not taken from the dough, it must be taken from the bread. *Hallah* can no longer be observed today as a priestly offering since there is no longer a temple in Jerusalem with a functioning Jewish priesthood. In order for the mitzvah not to be forgotten, traditional Jewish housewives today in preparing bread are bidden to throw a small portion of it (the size of an olive) into the oven. This is accompanied by this benediction: Praised are You, Adonai our God, Ruler of the Universe who has made us holy by your mitzvot and commanded us to set aside *hallah*.

Today the name *hallah* is applied to the Sabbath loaves, from which *hallah* has presumably been set aside. It is also customary to set aside something for charity in conjunction with the removal of *hallah*.

4

BAN ON LEAVEN ON PASSOVER

On the first day [of Passover], you shall put away leaven out of your house.

—Exodus 12:15

In the first month, on the fourteenth day of the month, in the evening, you shall eat unleavened bread.

—Exodus 12:18

Seven days shall there be no leaven in your houses.

—Exodus 12:19

DETAILS

To prepare for the festival of Passover, one is biblically commanded to remove all leaven (*chametz*) from one's home and eat only unleavened bread (matzah) during the holiday. Jewish law requires that all leaven must be removed from the home on the fourteenth of the month of Nisan (eve of Passover). *Chametz* includes any food derived from wheat, spelt, barley, rye, or oats.

BAN ON LEAVEN ON PASSOVER IN A NUTSHELL

Jewish law demands that all Jewish persons eat matzah on the first night of Passover. During the rest of the festival, one is encouraged to eat it and certainly forbidden from eating any leaven during all the festival.

The official search for leaven in one's home occurs at the beginning of the fourteenth of Nisan, following an elaborate cleaning of the house in preparation for the festival of Passover. The searching is performed symbolically by deliberately placing crumbs of bread in several parts of the house and then discovering and sweeping them into a wooden spoon which is wrapped in a cloth and burning them in the morning on the eve of Passover.

Today, to be certain that a Jewish family does not have leaven in its possession, the rabbis instituted the custom of "selling the leaven" to a non-Jew for the duration of the festival.

In his allegorical explanation of the ban on leaven, the commentator Bachya ben Asher compares leaven to stern judgment. Just as leaven expands and spreads out, so too does judgment expand and not retreat. Thus, we must remove all leaven from our homes when we celebrate the festival of freedom. This teaches that life itself must be based on mercy, compassion, and kindness, and not only on strict judgment.

5

BILAAM'S TALKING DONKEY

Bilaam rose up in the morning, and saddled his ass, and went with the princes of Moab. And God's anger was kindled because he went, and the angel of the Lord placed himself in the way for an adversary against him. Now he was riding his ass, and his two servants were with him. And the ass saw the angel of the Lord standing in the way, with his sword drawn in his hand. And the ass turned aside out of the way, and went into the field. And Bilaam smote the ass to turn her into the way . . . And the ass saw the angel of the Lord, and she thrust herself unto the wall, and crushed Bilaam's foot against the wall, and he smote her again . . . And the Lord opened the mouth of the ass, and she said to Bilaam: "What have I done to you, that you have smitten me these three times?" And Bilaam said to the ass: "Because you have mocked me; I would there were a sword in my hand, for now I had killed you." And the ass said to Bilaam: "Am I not your ass, upon which you have ridden all your life long unto this day? Have I been in the habit of doing thus to you?" And he answered, "No."

—Numbers 22: 22–30

DETAILS

In this most incredible Bible story, the pagan prophet Bilaam was sent by Balak, King of the Moabites, to put a curse on the Israelites. Belief in the power of curses was very strong in biblical times, and even God viewed Bilaam's intent with grave alarm. As Bilaam was riding on his donkey, the donkey caught sight of God's angel standing in the way with drawn sword. The donkey swerved from the road and went into the field, and Bilaam beat it to return. After several beatings with a stick, God opened the mouth of the donkey and it spoke.

BILAAM'S TALKING DONKEY IN A NUTSHELL

Traditional Jewish commentators have considered the speaking donkey that rebukes Bilaam a miraculous wonder and its speech a wonder designed to magnify God's name and to demonstrate God's eternal love of the children of Israel. It is God who gives and controls speech, both in humans and animals. Maimonides, the medieval commentator, tried to rationalize the intent of the story, holding the opinion that Bilaam experienced the whole episode as a vision and that it really did not happen. Even more amazing than the donkey speaking is the miraculous fact that it perceived the angel of God, whereas Bilaam the prophet did not.

The lampooning of Bilaam in this Bible story by the use of a talking donkey not only serves to downgrade his reputation but to demonstrate that one who was intent on putting a curse on the Israelites without the expressed consent of God was nothing more than a fool.

6

BLESSING ONE'S FOOD

When you have eaten your fill, give thanks to God for the good land which God has given you.

—Deuteronomy 8:10

DETAILS

The *Birkat Hamazon*, the grace after the meal, is recited after any meal that began with the blessing over bread (*hamotzi*). It consists of four benedictions or paragraphs, three of which are of high antiquity. The fourth, of later origin, was instituted after Bar Kochba's defeat, about 135 of the common era.

According to a talmudic statement (*Berachot* 48b), the first paragraph was composed by Moses, the second by his successor Joshua, the third by David and Solomon, and the fourth by the sages. The first is an acknowledgment of God as the sustainer of all creatures. The second is a thanksgiving for the grant of the Torah and the Land of Israel. The third paragraph is a prayer for the restoration of Zion and Jerusalem. The fourth paragraph is an expression of gratitude for the general benefits and favors bestowed on man by his Creator.

There is an introductory formula to the *Birkat Hamazon*, used when three or more people recite the grace jointly, which is taken

11

from the Mishnah of *Berachot* 7:3. The duty of inviting the table companions to jointly recite the blessing after the meal is based on Psalm 34:4: "Exalt the Lord with me, and let us extol the Lord together."

BLESSING ONE'S FOOD IN A NUTSHELL

The blessing after the meal is recited after any meal that began with the blessing over bread (*hamotzi*). When at least three people eat together, they constitute a *mezuman*. One of the three is asked to call the others to say the *Birkat Hamazon* through an introductory formula that begins *Rabbotai nevarech* ("let us say grace"). It is the usual custom to give the honor of leading the blessing after the meal to a guest.

Before the blessing after the meal, some people have the custom of removing all utensils (especially knives) from the table and leaving a piece of bread (or crumbs) on the table. Knives were used as weapons of war, and the table is considered an altar of peace and tranquility.

After eating food consisting of cake, wine, and so forth (without bread), there is a special blessing called *beracha acharona* that is recited. It is a sort of abridged version of *Birkat Hamazon*.

Here is the first paragraph of the blessing after the meal:

Praised are You, our God, Sovereign of the Universe, who sustains the whole world with kindness and compassion. God provides food for every creature, for God's love endures forever. God's great goodness has never failed us. God's great glory assures us nourishment. All life is God's creation and God is good to all, providing every creature with food and sustenance. Praised are You, God, who sustains life.

7
BURNING BUSH

Now Moses was keeping the flock of Jethro his father-in-law, the priest of Midian. He led the flock to the farthest end of the wilderness, and came to the mountain of God, unto Horeb. And the angel of the Lord appeared to him in a flame of fire out of the midst of the bush. And he looked, and behold, the bush burned with fire, and the bush was not consumed. And Moses said: "I will turn aside now and see this great sight, why the bush is not burnt." And when the Lord saw that he turned aside to see, God called unto him out of the midst of the bush and said: "Here am I." And God said: "Draw not near. Put off your shoes from your feet, for the place upon which you are standing is holy ground."

—Exodus 3:1–5

DETAILS

It was in the desert wilderness while tending his flock that Moses first experienced the wondrous and commanding presence of God. An angel of God pointed Moses in the direction of the burning bush that was not consumed by its own fire.

13

Biblical commentators have noted that in the story of the burning bush, God may have been testing Moses' attention span. Perhaps the bush was designed merely to attract Moses' attention, to make him look and stare, to shock and prepare him for what was to come. Or the bush may have been symbolic, subject both to a general and detailed interpretation.

BURNING BUSH IN A NUTSHELL

According to the rabbis in the midrash, God never gives an exalted office to a man unless He has first tested him in small things. Perhaps this was the purpose of the burning bush—to allow Moses time to examine this miraculous sight and realize that something very special was happening in this place.

Some commentators have suggested that the bush symbolized puny Israel, threatened with destruction by the fire of Egyptian persecution. Other commentators have suggested that the lowly bush was presented as God's fire to show Moses that there is no place without God's presence, not even a thornbush. Whatever the case, Moses clearly seemed to get the message. By saying *hineni*—"here I am" (reminiscent of Abraham who answered similarly when told by God's angel to put down his knife and to not sacrifice his son Isaac) Moses indicated that he was prepared to listen to God and to learn of the mission that he would be asked to execute.

8
BUSINESS ETHICS

You shall not oppress a hired servant that is poor and needy, whether he be of your brethren, or of your strangers that are in your land within your gates. In the same day you shall give him his wages.

—Deuteronomy 24:14–15

DETAILS

The Bible was careful to warn employers not to oppress the poor and needy. The workman was not to be wronged by being kept waiting for his wage. It had to be punctually paid to him on the day that he earned it.

There are numerous rabbinic statements and stories regarding the importance of taking care of the worker. In the following famous anecdote about the sage Rabbah and his careless porters, we see the great concern for the welfare of working people and the importance of taking on responsibilities beyond the strict letters of the law in order to treat the worker with kindness:

Some porters carelessly dropped a barrel of wine they were carrying for Rabbah bar Chana. As a penalty, he took their coats away from them. The men went to Rav and complained and he ordered their coats be returned.

15

"Is that the law?" Rabbah asked (knowing that he had the law on his side).

"It is," answered Rav, "because the Bible says: 'That you may walk in the way of good people'" (Proverbs 2:20).

After their coats were returned, the workmen said, "We are poor people who worked all day, and we are hungry. Are we not entitled to get paid?"

"Pay them," Rav ordered.

"Is that the law?" asked Rabbah (surprised that he should be ordered to pay such careless people).

"It is," came the answer, "for it is written: 'And keep the paths of righteousness'" (*Baba Metzia* 83a).

BUSINESS ETHICS IN A NUTSHELL

A famous rabbinic saying is that of the fourth century Babylonian teacher Rava. Rava said that on Judgment Day the first question God asks a man is: "Were you reliable in your business dealings?"

Even though in rabbinic times there were no great corporations or industry because society was by and large an agricultural one, there were a plethora of ethical principles governing business relations. In rabbinic law, for example, an overcharge (or undercharge) of more than one-sixth of the value of a commodity invalidated the sale (Talmud *Baba Metzia* 30b). When goods were sold, it was the delivery of the goods that established the sale and not payment. Consequently, if a man had paid for some commodity that had not yet been delivered, either party could back out of the deal without the courts compelling him to abide by it.

In the talmudic tractate of *Sanhedrin* (81a), to take away a person's livelihood by unfair competition is compared to adultery. In modern times numerous tales have been told of the exemplary business integrity of Rabbi Israel Meir Ha-Kohen (1838–1933), known as the Hafez Hayyim (after the title of his first book). Even if some of these tales are legendary, the fact remains that the Hafez Hayyim, though an outstanding talmudist, occupied no official rabbinic position, preferring to earn his living in commerce (along with Jewish law) with extraordinary devotion to the highest ideals of honesty.

9

CANDELABRUM—MENORAH

And you shall command the children of Israel, that they bring to you pure olive oil, beaten for the light, to cause a lamp to burn continually.

—Exodus 27:20

DETAILS

The seven-branched candelabrum, the menorah, used in the portable sanctuary set up by Moses in the wilderness as well as in the Jerusalem Temple, consisted of a base and a shaft with six branches, beaten out of solid gold. The six branches curved to the height of the central shaft, so that all the seven lamps, symbolizing the ideal of universal enlightenment, were in a straight line. They were provided daily with fresh olive oil of the purest quality, and they burned from evening to morning (Exodus 27:1).

CANDELABRUM—MENORAH— IN A NUTSHELL

According to the historian Josephus, three of the seven lamps of the menorah were allowed to burn by day. According to Jewish tradition, however, only the center lamp was left burning all day. It was called the Western Lamp (*Ner Ha-Ma'aravi*) because it was next to the branches on the east side. The Western Lamp is also referred to as *Ner Elohim* (the lamp of God), mentioned in I Samuel 3:3, which is represented in the synagogue by the *Ner Tamid*, the eternal light burning above the Holy Ark.

The menorah also symbolizes the creation of the universe in seven days, the center light representing the Sabbath. The seven branches are also said to allude to the continents of the earth as well as the seven heavens, guided by the light of God.

Frequently used as a symbol of Judaism and the Jewish people, a representation of the seven-branched candelabrum has been found on many tombs and monuments dating from the first century.

The earliest preserved and most authentic representation of the temple menorah is depicted on the arch of Titus commemorating the triumphal parade following the destruction of Jerusalem in the year 70. According to a talmudic statement (*Menachot* 28b), it is prohibited to use a seven-branched menorah outside the temple.

10
CAPITAL PUNISHMENT

He that strikes a person so that he dies shall surely be put to death.

—Exodus 21:12

DETAILS

Prescribing capital punishment for a variety of offenses in biblical times was believed to be a deterrent and justified by the fact that the perpetrator was detrimental to the community because, in a sense, he had offended God. Under Jewish law, capital punishment was imposed only when the Jerusalem Temple was in existence. Rabbinic authorities made every effort to have judges avoid imposing capital punishment. We are told in the talmudic tractate of *Sanhedrin* 63a that the members of a court that pronounced a capital sentence were obliged to abstain from all food on the day of execution.

Perhaps the most important passage in rabbinic literature regarding capital punishment is found in the Mishnah of Makkot 1:10:

A Sanhedrin which executes a criminal once in seven years is known as destructive. Rabbi Eleazar son of Azariah says: Once in seventy years. Rabbi Tarfon and Rabbi Akiva say: If we had been members of the Sanhedrin no man would ever have been executed. Rabban Simeon son of Gamaliel says: They [Rabbi Tarfon and Rabbi Akiba] would have been responsible for the proliferation of murderers in Israel.

CAPITAL PUNISHMENT IN A NUTSHELL

In the Torah, the death penalty was prescribed for many different crimes including murder, adultery, blasphemy, false evidence in capital cases, false prophecy, idolatry, incest, striking one's parents, profaning the Sabbath, and witchcraft. The four major types of capital punishment known in bygone years were death by strangling, sword, fire, and stoning.

In the case of only causing injury to another person (that is Exodus 21:18), the injured was entitled to compensation based on loss of time from work and medical treatment. Rabbinic law expanded compensation to include compensation for physical disability, pain, and indignity.

Modern Israel has no capital punishment except for participation in genocidal activities and under certain conditions of warfare.

11

GETTING INVOLVED WHEN YOU SEE A CRIME— LAW OF THE GOOD SAMARITAN

Do not stand idly by the blood of your neighbor.

—Leviticus 19:16

DETAILS

The biblical commandment of not standing idly by when a crime is being perpetrated suggests that people need to be involved when they see a wrong being committed. This commandment has been rabbinically understood in the field of medical ethics as justifying the destruction of an embryo in a woman's womb to save her life. In such a case, the embryo is regarded as the "pursuer," the mother as the victim, and the doctor as the rescuer.

GETTING INVOLVED WHEN YOU SEE A CRIME IN A NUTSHELL

Jewish opinion has always recommended involvement when one sees a crime being perpetrated upon another. The great commentator the Hinnuch comments that the root purpose of this commandment is self-evident. Just as one person will save his fellow human being, so will the other save him when necessary. This makes for the kind of world in which people help one another, and in this kind of society does God truly delight.

Perhaps the law of getting involved when one sees a crime can be best summed up in this famous rabbinic adage: "One who saves one person in Israel, it is as if that person saved the entire world."

12

CHERUBIM

To the east of the garden of Eden God placed the cherubim.

—Genesis 3:24

You shall make two cherubim *of gold; of beaten work you shall make them, at the two ends of the ark cover. And make one cherub at the one end, and one cherub at the other end; of one piece with the ark cover shall you make the* cherubim *of the two ends thereof. And the cherubim shall spread out their wings on high, screening the ark cover with their wings, with their faces one to another.*

—Exodus 25:18–22

DETAILS

The Bible frequently refers to *cherubim*—a type of celestial being—to be distinguished from cherubs, those adoring, chubby, winged infants with rosy cheeks that fly around in Western art. The etymology of the Hebrew word for cherub, *keruv*, has been subject to different interpretations. The Tur Sinai, a Bible commentator, explained that the word *keruv* was derived from the Aramaic *karov*, meaning "to plow," which is based on Ezekiel's substitution of the face of a cherub (10:14) for that of an ox (1:10) whose main function is to plow. Others have commented that the word *keruv* is derived from the Akkadian *karabu*, meaning "to pray or to bless." Thus a cherub serves as an intermediary who brings the prayers of humans to the gods.

CHERUBIM IN A NUTSHELL

Figures of winged creatures were well known in the art of the ancient Near East, appearing on pottery incense altars from Megiddo as well as flanking the throne of Hiram, king of Byblos. In the Bible, *cherubim* appear for the first time as guardians of the garden of Eden after Adam and Eve were expelled. The purpose of these beings was to guard the way to the tree of life.

In the desert tabernacle, hammered golden *cherubim* faced each other on the cover of the Ark of the Covenant (Exodus 25:18–22; 37:7–9). They are described as facing one another on the two ends of the covering above the Ark of the Covenant, forming the throne of God with their outstretched wings. They are the counterparts of two very large *cherubim* found in the Holy of Holies of King Solomon's temple.

Faces of the *cherubim* were also used for decorative purposes. In Exodus 26:31, they are described as having been embroidered on the veil separating the holy place from the most Holy, on the tabernacle curtains (Exodus 26:1), and carved both on the inner and outer walls and the doors of the inner and outer sanctuary (I Kings 6:29, 32, 35).

The question of how images such as *cherubim* could have had a place in the Israelite cult, which is generally imageless, has not been satisfactorily answered. It has been conjectured that the *cherubim* belonged to an old mythological tradition that was unable to be dislodged, and hiding them away in a place such as the Holy of Holies minimized their accessibility and thus the danger of worshipping them. In any event, by the time of the destruction of the First Temple in 586 B.C.E., they disappeared and were not reconstructed when the Second Temple was built.

13

THE CHOSEN PEOPLE OF ISRAEL

*You have seen what I did to the Egyptians, and how I bore
you on eagle's wings and brought you to Me. Now, therefore,
if you will listen to Me and keep My covenant, then you
shall be My own treasure from all peoples. For all the earth
is Mine. And you shall be to Me a kingdom of priests and
a holy nation.*

—Exodus 19:4-6

*God has chosen you to be God's treasure from all of the
peoples that are upon the face of the earth. God did not set
His love upon you, nor choose you, because you were more in
number than any other people—for you were the fewest of
all peoples—but because God loved you.*

—Deuteronomy 7:6–8

DETAILS

The idea that the Jewish people were specially selected by God
to carry out some special purpose is prominent throughout the
Bible and in other Jewish teachings. Many people have questioned

God's relationship to the Jews, often wondering how it is possible that God would choose to have a favorite people, namely the Jews, and give other peoples lesser roles in the divine plan for humanity. A poet once put in this way:

> How odd
> Of God
> To choose
> The Jews

Here we see the poet calling attention to two matters. One is that God, the supposed Parent of all peoples, chose a particular people to be His own. The other is how surprising it is that God would select the Jews as the particular people.

In a statement from the prophet Amos, we learn the following: "You alone have I singled out of all the families of the earth. That is why I call you to account for all of your iniquities" (Amos 3:2). From this statement we can conclude that chosenness does not endow Jews with special rights in the way that racist ideologies endow those born into the "superior" race.

The prophet Isaiah further expands upon the concept of chosenness:

> I am God, I have called you in righteousness . . .
> I have given you as a covenant to the people.
> For a light to the nations,
> To open the eyes that are blind.
>
> —Isaiah 42:6–7

Here we clearly see that according to the prophet, the Jewish people has been assigned the mission of improving the world and teaching other peoples to see the light. Chosenness is thus not a privilege of which to boast but rather a task to be undertaken. For Jewish people, it means contributing to the betterment of the world, what the Jewish tradition calls *tikkun olam*—"repairing the world." It means increased responsibilities and hardship.

CHOSEN PEOPLE OF ISRAEL IN A NUTSHELL

For the Jewish people chosenness does not mean that the Jews have been singled out for special favors. Rather, according to the prophetic teachings, it means that the Jews have been selected to carry out the special duties of being God's partner and servant, helping to bring about a just and good world.

The best thinking by various Jewish theologians on the subject of the election of Israel may well be summed up as follows. Only in Israel did ethical monotheism exist. Wherever else it is found later on, it has been derived directly or indirectly from Israel. The term "election of Israel" thus merely expresses a historical fact. Israel feels itself chosen, not as master but as servant. It separates itself from others only for the purpose of uniting them. The people of Israel affirm not that they are better than others, but that they ought to be better.

David Ben-Gurion, former Prime Minister of Israel, once said, "We are the chosen people only if we choose to be so."

14
CIRCUMCISION

God said to Abraham: As for you, you and your offspring to come throughout the ages shall keep My covenant. Such shall be the covenant between Me and you and your offspring to follow which you shall keep: every male among you shall be circumcised. You shall circumcise the flesh of your foreskin and that shall be the sign of the covenant between Me and you. And throughout the generations, every male among you shall be circumcised at the age of eight days.

—Genesis 17:9–12

DETAILS

Circumcision is the characteristic symbol of Judaism and is its oldest ritual. Abraham was instructed to have himself circumcised at the age of ninety-nine. The ceremony, which involves removing the foreskin of the penis, continues to be performed on Jewish male infants at the age of eight days.

Circumcision was taken as such an important religious obligation that when King Antiochus prohibited circumcision more than two thousand years ago, the Jews were ready to die rather than abandon it.

The mohel (ritual circumcisor) is subject to regulations that ensure the performance of the operation with adequate precautions. The main participants in the circumcision ceremony are the father and mother of the child and the mohel. Others include the sandek, whose privilege it is to hold the child during the circumcision. There are also godparents, called the kvater and kvaterin, whose role it is to hand the infant to the mohel. The Prophet Elijah is the invisible participant at circumcisions, being referred to as "the angel of the covenant" (Malachi 3:1) and protector of children. A special chair or pillow is reserved for him.

CIRCUMCISION IN A NUTSHELL

The circumcision of a Jewish male infant must take place on the eighth day, even if that day is the Sabbath or Day of Atonement. (Postponement is permitted only when the health of the child would be endangered.) The chief participants in the ritual, in addition to the child, are the mohel (performer of the rite), the parents, the sandek (holds the child during the ritual), and the godparents (kvater and kvaterin). The parents of the infant recite this blessing following the circumcision.

> Baruch atah Adonai elohaynu melech ha'olam asher kidshanu bemitzvotav vetzivanu le'hachneeso shel Avraham avinu.

> Praised are You, Adonai our God, Ruler of the universe who has made us holy with mitzvot and instructed us to bring our son into the covenant of Abraham our father.

All those present then respond:

Keshem she'neechnas labrit, ken yikanes letorah, ulchuppah, ulema'asim tovim.

As he has entered the covenant, so may he attain the blessings of Torah, marriage, and a life of good deeds.

The officiant then pronounces the blessing over a cup of wine and proceeds to give the baby boy his Hebrew name.

15
CITIES OF REFUGE

And God spoke to Moses in the plains of Moab the Jordan at Jericho, saying: "Command the children of Israel, that they give to the Levites of the inheritance of their possession cities to dwell in; and open land round about the cities shall you give to the Levites. And the cities shall they have to dwell in, and their open land shall be for their cattle, and for their substance, and for all their beasts. And the open land about the cities, which you shall give to the Levites, shall be from the wall of the city and outward a thousand cubits around about. And you shall measure without the city for the east side two thousand cubits, and for the south side two thousand cubits, and for the west side two thousand cubits, and for the north side two thousand cubits, the city being in the midst. This shall be to them the open land about the cities. And the cities which you shall give to the Levites, they shall be the six cities of refuge, which you shall give for the manslayer to flee there. And beside them shall you give forty-two cities . . . And the cities shall be to you for refuge from the avenger, that the manslayer not die, until he stands before the congregation for judgment."

—Numbers 35: 1–7; 12

33

DETAILS

In biblical times, the right and duty to avenge a murder belonged to the close relatives of the slain. The cities of refuge were designed to shelter anyone who might accidentally commit man-slaughter. By fleeing into one of the cities of refuge, persons pursued by avengers of blood were protected against the ancient law of life for a life. Forty-two Levitical cities also served for the protection of unintentional homicide. Anyone killing a man and fleeing to one of those cities was granted a fair trial and was not put to death unless he had committed actual murder.

CITIES OF REFUGE IN A NUTSHELL

In primitive society, shame rested upon the family until its nearest representative, called "blood redeemer" (*go'el ha-dam*), even-tually killed the man responsible for the death of one of its members. He slew him without any preliminary trial to settle the actual facts of the case. Then, it often happened, the nearest relative of the second man slain murdered the blood avenger, and a blood feud was established. The system, which prevailed among the Semites and other nations including the ancient Greeks, was de-stroyed by the Bible's legislation, assigning the decision of the guilt of the innocence of the manslayer to an impartial court of justice.

The cities of refuge described in the Bible provided places of asylum in which an accidental killer was to be safe from the vengeance of the murdered man's kinsmen, and where he was required to stay until the death of the reigning high priest. This is explained in the Talmud to the effect that the exiled man gains his freedom through the death of the high priest, because the high priest should have prevented the calamity in Israel by virtue of prayer. Hence, only his death expiates the homicide's sin (Talmud *Makkot* 11a). The inviolability of the refuges is expressly repudiated in cases of willful murder.

16
CIVIL DISOBEDIENCE

The Egyptians made the children of Israel to serve with rigor. And they made their lives bitter with hard service, in mortar and in brick, and in all manner of service in the field. And the king of Egypt spoke to the Hebrew midwives, of whom the name of the one was Shiphrah and the name of the other Puah. And he said: "When you do the office of a midwife to the Hebrew women, you shall look upon the birthstool. If it be a son, then you shall kill him. But if it be a daughter, then shall she live." But the midwives feared God, and did not as the king of Egypt commanded them, but saved the male children alive.

—Exodus 1:13–17

And it came to pass in those days, when Moses was grown up, that he went out to his brethren, and looked on their burdens, and he saw an Egyptian smiting a Hebrew, one of his brethren. And he looked this way and that way, when he saw that there was no man, he smote the Egyptian, and hid him in the sand.

—Exodus 2:11–12

DETAILS

In the first biblical source, Shifra and Puah, the Hebrew midwives, are the first to demonstrate justified civil disobedience in the Bible. They defy Pharaoh's orders in which he commands the death of Israelite children.

It is clear from the second passage of the biblical sources that where the practices of the governing body are iniquitous, they should be resisted. When Moses observes an Egyptian taskmaster mercilessly flogging a Hebrew slave, he has no compunction about slaying the Egyptian.

CIVIL DISOBEDIENCE IN A NUTSHELL

There are a plethora of Jewish sources to support the importance of resisting the demands of a tyrannical government. For example, there is a statement in the Talmudic tractate of *Nedarim* 3:4 dating from Temple times that says "if murderers, robbers, or tax collectors" wish to seize one's goods, it is permitted to take a false oath to the effect that the goods belong to the king's household to frighten them off.

The difficulty in most of the situations in which civil disobedience is advocated is to determine when a government is tyrannical and iniquitous. Jews living in democracies have to be especially careful in assessing the rights and wrongs of civil disobedience.

17
COMPASSION TOWARD ANIMALS

The seventh day is a Sabbath unto the Lord your God: you shall not do any work, you, your son or daughter, your male or female servant, or your cattle.

—Exodus 20:10

You shall not plow with an ox and mule harnessed together. (An ox and a mule are of unequal size and strength, and will suffer as a result of being harnessed together).

—Deuteronomy 22:10

If along the road you come upon a bird's nest, with fledglings or eggs and the mother sitting over the fledglings or on the eggs, do not take the mother together with her young. Let the mother fly away and only then take the young.

—Deuteronomy 22:6–7

No animal shall be slaughtered on the same day with its young.

—Leviticus 22:28

When you see your enemy's donkey lying under its load and would like to leave it alone, you must nevertheless help it get on its feet.

—Exodus 23:5

For the blood is the life, and you shall not eat the life with the flesh. You shall pour it upon the earth as water.

—Deuteronomy 12:23

DETAILS

Already in biblical times we find several laws that teach us compassion for animals. The religious obligation of observing Sabbath rest (the fourth of the Ten Commandments) is extended to our animals too: ox, donkey, and cattle.

Maimonides, the medieval philosopher, has the following to say regarding the biblical law forbidding the slaughter of an animal with its young on the same day:

It is prohibited to kill an animal and its young in such a manner that the young is slain in the sight of its mother, for the pain of the animals under such circumstances is very great. There is no difference in this case between the pain of a man and the pain of other living beings, since the love and tenderness of the mother for her young ones exist not only in man but in most living beings.

The same reason applies to the law that obligates us to let the mother fly away when we take the young. If the law provides that such grief not be caused to cattle or birds, how much more careful must we be not to cause grief to our fellow man (*Guide to the Perplexed*, 3:48).

The Talmud also assumes that animals suffer more than human beings from hunger, presumably because an animal that has not been fed has no idea if it ever will be fed. Thus follows the rabbinic injunction that a person is prohibited to eat until he or she first feeds one's animals (Talmud *Berachot* 40a).

COMPASSION TOWARD ANIMALS IN A NUTSHELL

In general, both the Bible and rabbinic law gave extraordinary emphasis on compassion for animals. The Jewish dietary laws guaranteed that an animal was permitted as food only if it was slaughtered quickly so that death was instantaneous. All animals killed through hunting were unkosher.

There are some rabbinic commentators that have read into biblical passages the ideal of vegetarianism as a way of life. In the creation narrative (Genesis 29:30), for instance, both man and the animals are given the herbs of the field for their food and they were not to prey on one another. Adam, the ideal man, an inhabitant of the Garden of Eden, is limited to eating only fruits and vegetables. Just as at the beginning of time, in the perfect society as symbolized by the Garden of Eden, there was no eating of meat, so at the end of time, in the perfect society as described by the Prophet Isaiah, there will be a return to the original state:

> And the wolf will dwell with the lamb
> And the leopard shall lie down with the kid.
> And the calf and the young lion and the fatling together.
> —Isaiah 11:6–7

Indeed, the biblical permission to eat meat appears to be a sort of Divine compromise. That is to say, meat is permissible for consumption, but people must learn to have reverence for the life of the flesh that is taken.

This story in the Talmud (*Baba Metzia* 85a) offers a fine summary of the rabbinic attitude toward care of animals:

Rabbi Judah the Prince observed a calf as it was being led to the slaughterhouse. The animal broke away from the herd and hid itself under Rabbi Judah's clothing, crying for mercy. But Judah pushed it away saying, "Go. This is your destiny." They said in heaven: "Since he showed no compassion, we will bring suffering to him." For many years after this act, Rabbi Judah suffered a series of painful illnesses. One day, Judah's servant was sweeping the house. She was about to sweep away some young weasels which she found on the floor. "Leave them alone," Judah said to the housekeeper. Subsequently they spoke of Judah this way in heaven, "Since he has shown compassion to these rodents, we will be compassionate with him" and he was cured of his illnesses.

18
CURSING

You shall not curse a judge, and a rule of your people you shall not revile.

—Exodus 22:27

You shall not curse a deaf person.

—Leviticus 19:14

DETAILS

Among ancient and primitive peoples, a curse was more than an expressed wish for evil. It was considered a method of making the potential harm become a reality. Curses were often pronounced in the name of a god or demon. Belief in the power of curses was most prevalent among the ancient Babylonians, who relied on professional sorcerers to curse their enemies before battle.

The commentator the Hinnuch states that when a person curses a judge, he defies not only the court, but God Himself, since the court is acting in God's name. Maimonides is of the opinion that although a curse cannot really harm one's victim, it is forbidden to curse because the desire to curse someone is usually a result of some pent-up feeling of anger or hurt. Thus, the prohibition against cursing is an attempt to wean a person from feelings of anger.

CURSING IN A NUTSHELL

The Bible approaches the act of cursing with great seriousness. When Bilaam, the Moabite prophet (Numbers 25), prepares to curse the Israelites, God makes sure that his curse will be deflected and turned into a blessing.

Under biblical law, one who used God's name for purposes of cursing was subject to execution by stoning.

19
DIETARY LAWS

You shall not cook a kid in its mother's milk.

> —Exodus 23:19; 34:26; Deuteronomy 14:21

Since the life of a living body is in its blood . . . no one among you may eat blood.

> —Leviticus 17:11–12

You shall set apart the [ritually] clean beast from the unclean.

> —Leviticus 20:25

You must not eat flesh torn by beasts.

> —Exodus 22:30

You shall not eat anything that died a natural death.

> —Deuteronomy 14:21

DETAILS

A detailed account of permissible and nonpermissible animals is provided in the eleventh chapter of the Book of Leviticus:

God spoke to Moses and to Aaron, saying to them: These are the things that you may eat among all the beasts that are on the earth. Whatsoever parts the hoof, and is wholly cloven-footed, and chews the cud, among the beasts, that may you eat. Nevertheless, these shall you not eat of them that only chew the cud, or of them that only part the hoof: the camel, because he chews the cud but does not part the hoof, he is unclean to you. And the rockbadger, because he chews the cud but does not part the hoof, he is unclean to you. And the hare, because she chews the cud but does not part the hoof, she is unclean to you. And the swine, because he parts the hoof and is cloven-footed, but does not chew the cud, he is unclean to you. Of their flesh you shall not eat, and their carcasses you shall not touch; they are unclean to you. These you may eat of all that are in the waters: whatsoever has fins and scales in the waters, in the seas and in the rivers, you may eat. And all that do not have fins and scales in the waters, seas and river, you may not eat them. And all that have not fins and scales in the seas, and in the rivers, of all that swarm in the waters, and of all the living creatures that are in the waters, they are a detestable thing to you. Whatsoever has no fins or scales in the waters, that is a detestable thing to you. And these you shall have in detestation among the fowls: they shall not be eaten: the great vulture, and the bearded vulture, and the osprey. And the kite, and the falcon after its kinds. Every raven after its kinds. And the ostrich and nighthawk, and the sea-mew and the hawk after its kinds. And the little owl, and the cormorant, and the great owl. And the horned owl, and the pelican, and the carrion-vulture. And the stork and the heron after its kinds, and the hoopoe and the bat. All winged swarming things that go upon all fours are a detestable thing to you. Yet these may you eat of swarming things that go upon all fours, which have jointed legs above their feet, wherewith to leap upon the earth. Even these of them you may eat: the locust after its kinds, and the cricket after its kinds, and the grasshopper after its kinds. But all winged swarming things, which have four feet, are a detestable thing to you . . . For I am Adonai your God. Sanctify yourselves and be holy, for I am holy. Neither shall you defile yourselves with any manner of swarming thing that moves upon the earth. For I am Adonai your God that brought you up out of the land of Egypt, to be your God. You shall therefore be holy, for I am holy. This is the law of the beast, and of the fowl, and of every living creature that moves in the waters, and of every creature that swarms upon the earth. To make a difference between the unclean and the clean. And between the living thing that may be eaten and the living thing that may not be eaten (Leviticus 11:1-23, 44-47).

Chapters 11 through 16 of the Book of Leviticus contain the laws of purity. Among the laws of purity, first place is given to the subject of food, because one's daily diet affects a person's whole being.

The Hebrew term *kashrut* "fitness" is generally applied to things and persons that meet Jewish religious requirements. For the most part the term is used in the sense of food ritually clean and edible. According to the Bible, animals that have parted hooves and chew their cuds (oxen, sheep, goats, and certain deer, just to name a few examples) are permissible. Aquatic animals that lack fins and scales, such as eels, are forbidden. Animals that are torn by another animal are forbidden, and animals that die of themselves are forbidden. The Bible also tells us that if a permissible animal is to be eaten, its blood must be properly drained. Furthermore, the Bible forbids the cooking of a kid in its mother's milk, which has been understood rabbinically to mean that one is not allowed to eat meat and dairy products together. Finally, birds of prey are strictly forbidden to be eaten as are a substantial number of insects.

Three times in the Bible the command is repeated not to boil a kid in its mother's milk. According to some, this was part of a Canaanite ritual, hence it is a prohibited pagan custom. This prohibition may also be intended to preserve the natural instinct of humanity and is symbolic of that considerate humanity which was to distinguish Israel from the barbarous nations. Rabbinically speaking, this commandment has been interpreted to mean that milk and meat cannot be eaten together or cooked together, and it is forbidden to derive benefit from food containing a milk and meat mixture. Rabbinic law also designed a waiting period between the eating of milk and meat. The period of waiting ranges from one to six hours, depending upon to which branch of Judaism one belongs. In addition, rabbinic law today has prescribed that all meat products must be certified kosher (that is, they have been ritually slaughtered according to prescribed rabbinic law). The slaying of animals for kosher food is controlled by regulations that ensure the minimum pain and the maximum effusion of blood in the animal. The remaining blood is extracted by means of washing, salting, and rinsing. It has been suggested that the purpose of all these may be to tame man's instincts of violence.

The subscription to chapter 11 of the Book of Leviticus (verses 43–47) reveals the object of the dietary laws. God brought Israel out of Egypt to be a holy and consecrated people, a people apart and distinguished from all others by outward rites, which in themselves helped to constitute holiness.

The deeply rooted observance of the Jewish dietary laws has, among other factors, prevented the Jews from being absorbed by the numerous nations in whose midst they have lived more than two thousand years. Hallowed since the days of Sinai, the dietary laws still are tenaciously kept by traditional Jewish people all over the world.

DIETARY LAWS IN A NUTSHELL

Meat

- All animals that chew their cud and have a split hoof are kosher.
- Meat must be killed according to the Jewish ritual laws of slaughtering, called "shechitah."
- Once the beast has been slaughtered, it must be properly salted to remove excess blood.

Eggs

- Eggs from nonkosher birds are not kosher.
- Eggs with bloodspots are not kosher.

Seafood

Fish that have fins and scales are permitted to be eaten.

Summary of Prohibited and Permitted Animals

Following is a partial list of permitted and prohibited animals, fowl, and seafood.

Animals

Prohibited

Permitted (have split hooves and chew their cud)

Prohibited	Permitted
horse	cattle
donkey	sheep
camel	goat
pig	deer
rabbit	

Fish and Seafood

Prohibited	Permitted
catfish	anchovy
eel	bluefish
porpoise	butterfish
shark	carp
whale	cod
clam	flounder
crab	fluke
frog	haddock
lobster	halibut
octopus	herring
oyster	mackerel
scallop	pike
	porgy
	red snapper
	salmon
	sardine
	seabass
	shad

Prohibited

shrimp
snail

Permitted

smelt
sole
trout
tuna
weakfish
whitefish

Fowl

Prohibited

bat
cuckoo
eagle
hawk
heron
kite
lapwing
ostrich
owl
pelican
stork
swan
vulture

Permitted

capon
chicken
dove
duck
geese
pigeon
turkey

20
Divorce

*When a man takes a wife and marries her, and it happens
that she finds no favor in his eyes, because he has found some
unseemly thing in her, then he writes her a bill of divorce.*

—Deuteronomy 24:1

DETAILS

Judaism exalts the sanctity of marriage and family life. Marriage is
seen as the ideal state in Jewish tradition. Yet, centuries ago, the
Jewish people recognized the possibility that a marital relationship
could fail, that two people may not be able to stay and live with each
other. Accordingly, provisions were made for the possibility of
divorce in biblical times. Though no specific divorcing couple is
mentioned in the Torah, it is clear that the practice existed and that
the Israelites had developed a legal means of handling what was
often a difficult and painful situation.

An entire talmudic volume called *Gittin* (*Divorces*) elaborates
the rabbinic specific details related to the divorce procedure.

DIVORCE IN A NUTSHELL

Jewish law has provided that a man can divorce his wife if:

- She refuses conjugal relations.
- She has no children after having been married ten years.
- She commits adultery.
- She is lax in religious observance.

In the year 1000 of the common era, Rabbi Gershom, an important Jewish legal authority, issued a famous edict that stated that a man may not divorce his wife except with her consent. Today in modern times, according to traditional Jewish law, a *get* (written bill of divorce) is required for every Jewish divorce. The *get* is written by a trained scribe and contains these components:

- A statement that the husband divorces his wife without duress.
- A statement that after the *get* the husband and wife may have no further sexual relationship.
- A time and place of the writing of the get.
- Complete Hebrew names of husband and wife, including any nicknames or added names by which they may be known.

21

DUTY TO HAVE CHILDREN— "BE FRUITFUL AND MULTIPLY"

Then God blessed them [Adam and Eve] and said: Be fruitful and multiply and fill the earth.

—Genesis 1:28

DETAILS

The first of the Bible's 613 commandments is that of having children, derived from God's command to Adam and Eve that they be fruitful and multiply. This biblical command has been rabbinically interpreted to mean that a couple should have two children, preferably one boy and one girl. This ruling is based on the following talmudic passage:

> A man may not refrain from fulfilling the commandment, "Be fruitful and multiply," unless he already has children. The School of Shammai ruled that he must have a minimum of two sons. The School of Hillel ruled: a son and a daughter, for it is written, "Male and female God created them" [Genesis 5:2] (Mishnah *Yevamot* 6:6).

Jewish law ruled according to the school of Hillel. A couple, where possible, should at least replace themselves (that is, they should have at least one child of each sex).

DUTY TO HAVE CHILDREN— "BE FRUITFUL AND MULTIPLY"— IN A NUTSHELL

On the sixth day of creation, having blessed the fish and the birds with fertility the day before, God blessed man and woman and said to them, "Be fruitful and multiply and replenish the earth" (Genesis 1:28). Not only is "be fruitful and multiply" one of Judaism's most important commandments, its theme repeats over and over again in the Bible. For instance, after the flood in the time of Noah, humanity is created and Noah is blessed with fertility (Genesis 9:1). Abraham, too, is to be blessed with progeny as numerous as the stars in the sky (Genesis 15:5).

In Judaism, having children is not only a religious obligation but one of the crowning achievements in the life of any husband and wife. So many customs and ceremonies are intended primarily for one's children that one can easily say with assurance that the child is the center of any Jewish home.

If a couple is unable to have children then the option of adopting a child comes into play. To adopt a child when one cannot have one's own is highly meritorious. This opinion is based on the rabbinic dictum that "whoever brings up an orphan in his home is regarded by the Bible as though the child had been born to him" (Talmud *Sanhedrin* 19b).

The high status of adoptive parents is also demonstrated in the following passage concerning a great Talmudic scholar:

Abbaye's father died when his mother conceived him, and his mother died when she bore him. But that is not so, for Abbaye used to say, "My mother told me." That was his adoptive mother (Talmud *Kiddushin* 31b).

22
ECOLOGY

When you shall besiege a city a long time, in making war against it, you shall not destroy the trees by wielding an ax against them, for you may eat of them, but you shall not cut them down . . . Only the trees of which you know that they are not trees for food, them you may destroy and cut down. [Here we see that even war does not justify needless destruction of the environment]

—Deuteronomy 20:19–21

You shall have a place also without the camp, wither you shall go forth abroad. And you shall have a paddle among your weapons. And it shall be, when you sit down abroad, you shall dig therewith and shall turn back and cover that which comes from you. [This source refers to the proper disposal of sewage]

—Deuteronomy 23:13–15

Six years you shall sow your land and gather in its yield. But in the seventh you shall let it rest and lie fallow. Let the needy among you eat of it.

—Exodus 23:10–11

DETAILS

Abeautiful legend in Ecclesiastes Rabbah 7:13 tells how God gave Adam a tour of the Garden of Eden, showing him all of its beauty. Then God said to Adam: "See how lovely and how worthy of praise are My works. They have been created for your sake. Take care not to spoil or destroy My world."

The message is a clear one. Adam and all humans to follow are given the task of being stewards of the world, the protectors of the environment.

The major legal principle of Jewish rabbinic law pertaining to ecology is that of *ba'al taschit* ("do not destroy"). This law is derived from the verse in Deuteronomy 20:19 that forbids the cutting of fruit-bearing trees. This precept serves as the basis for the talmudic law that prohibits willful destruction of natural resources or any kind of vandalism, even if the act is committed by the owners of the property.

Waste disposal was a major problem in rabbinic times. Care was taken that bits of broken glass should not be scattered on public land where they would cause injury. We are told that saintly men would bury their broken glassware deep in their own fields (Talmud *Baba Kamma* 30a).

According to the rabbis a tannery could not be set up in such a way that the prevailing winds could waft the unpleasant odor to the town. The Mishnah (*Baba Kamma* 7:7) ruled that goats or sheep must not be raised in the cultivated areas of the lands of Israel. This was a measure introduced to encourage renewed agricultural growth after the devastation to the land caused by the many wars with Rome.

An interesting piece of biblical environmental legislation is the establishment of a "migrash" or green belt around the cities. The Bible (Numbers 35:2–5 and Leviticus 25:34) speaks only of towns that were specifically assigned to the Levite:

Instruct the Israelite people to assign, out of the holdings apportioned to them, towns for the Levites to dwell in. You shall also assign to the Levites pasture land around their towns. The towns shall be theirs to dwell in, and the pasture shall be for the cattle they own and all their other beasts. The town pasture that you are to assign to the Levites shall extend a thousand cubits outside the town wall all around. You shall measure off two thousand cubits outside the town on the east side, two thousand on the south side, two thousand on the west side, and two thousand on the north side, with the town in the center. That shall be the pasture for their towns.

The philosopher Maimonides in his *Mishneh Torah* (Laws of the Sabbatical and Jubilee Years 13:6) expands the biblical ruling to include all cities. In a sense, the green belt became the precursor to modern environmental zoning regulations commonly seen in legislation today.

ECOLOGY IN A NUTSHELL

The religious obligation not to destroy is derived from the biblical verse that forbids the cutting down of fruit-bearing trees. The rabbis of the Talmud extended the principle prohibiting willful destruction of any object from which someone might benefit.

Jewish agricultural laws related to the Sabbatical Year provide for the needs of the land. The Bible (Exodus 23:11) declares that a Jewish farmer is permitted to sow and reap for six years, but the seventh year is set aside as a sabbath so that the earth may be renewed.

Indeed, the principle of do not destroy is rooted in the notion that "the earth is the Lord's and the fullness thereof" (Psalms 24:1). It is broadened in rabbinic law to include any gratuitous act of destruction:

Not only one who cuts down fruit trees, but also one who smashes household goods, tears clothes, demolishes a building, stops up a spring, or destroys food violates the command, "You must not destroy . . ." (Deuteronomy 20:19) (Moses Maimonides, *Mishneh Torah*, "Laws of Kings," 6:10).

23
Envy and Jealousy

You shall not be envious of your neighbor's wife, and you shall not covet your neighbor's house, or field, or servant, or anything that belongs to your neighbor.

—Exodus 20:14

DETAILS

In Judaism, covetousness takes one of two forms. First, a person casts a covetous eye upon the possessions (husband or wife, home, and so forth) of another individual, but his envy does not go beyond daydreaming. Although such envy is forbidden, these feelings are not subject to penalty, because they represent a violation of Jewish law in thought but not in deed. Second, there is the envy that leads to action. Here the coveting involves not only a desire for the possessions of another, but also devious attempts to talk the other person into giving up his possessions.

ENVY AND JEALOUSY IN A NUTSHELL

The only one of the Ten Commandments that deals with a person's feelings is related to envy. The only kind of envy that the rabbinic authorities not only tolerate but advocate is envy of those who study the Torah and practice its laws. Thus, one of their favorite sayings was: "The envy of scribes increases wisdom" (Talmud *Baba Batra* 21).

Here are some other rabbinic statements related to envy and jealousy that provide an excellent summary of the Jewish stance related to these concepts:

- Jealousy is as cruel as the grave (Song of Songs 8:6).
- Jealousy in the heart makes the bones rot (Proverbs 14:30).
- Envy, cupidity, and ambition drive a person from the world (Ethics of the Fathers 4:30).
- A person who is envious is guilty of robbery in thought (Rabbi Nachman of Bratslav).

24

Eye for an Eye

Eye for an eye, tooth for a tooth, hand for hand, foot for foot.

—Exodus 21:24

DETAILS

Few passages in the Bible have been so misunderstood as the one that states that injuries to life are to be met with punishments that reflect the seriousness of the crime. According to many biblical commentators, the biblical law of "an eye for an eye," which appears to lay down the principle of literal retribution, was not formulated for such a purpose. There are very few cases of physical retribution recorded in the Bible.

The law of "an eye for an eye" served to limit vengeance. It did not permit a life for an eye, or even two eyes for two eyes. The biblical principle suggested by it was that the punishment must be commensurate with the deed and never exceed it.

EYE FOR AN EYE IN A NUTSHELL

The ancient Code of Law of Hammurabi, hundreds of years older than the Torah, legislated retaliation even against innocent parties. Indeed during biblical times, blood feuds were practiced by many of Israel's neighbors.

The law of "an eye for an eye" always suggested that the punishment always be commensurate with the deed perpetrated.

By talmudic times, the rabbis understood and interpreted "an eye for an eye" to mean an eye for monetary compensation.

The biblical law of "an eye for an eye" represented an important stage in the development and extension of the sphere of criminal law and thereby had the important function of limiting private revenge, especially family or tribal feuds.

25
Family Blessings

The first source for the family blessings is Genesis 48:20. In this passage Jacob blesses his grandchildren Ephraim and Manasseh with these words: "By you shall Israel bless, saying: God make you as Ephraim and Manasseh."

The second source for the family blessings is the Book of Numbers 6:23–26. In this section God speaks to Moses who in turn is told to speak to his brother Aaron. God then presents Aaron with the blessing, which has come to be known as the three-fold priestly blessing:

> May God bless you and keep you.
> May God's Presence shine and be good to you.
> May God's face turn toward you and give you peace.

DETAILS

It is customary for Jewish parents to bless their children before sitting down to the Sabbath meal. The blessing provides parents with a privileged opportunity to express appreciation for their children. Through the touch of a parent's hand or the sound of a parent's voice, children can feel and respond to love and affection their family has for them.

The blessing for boys, derived from Genesis 48:20, invokes the shining example of Jacob's grandchildren Ephraim and Manasseh, who, although raised in Egypt, did not lose their identity as Jews. The traditional blessing for girls refers to the four matriarchs, Sarah, Rebekah, Rachel, and Leah, all of whom were known for their concern and compassion for others.

The family blessings conclude with the priestly benediction whose source is Numbers 6:23–26, invoking God's protection and peace.

FAMILY BLESSINGS IN A NUTSHELL

For boys, parents gently place both hands on his head and recite:

Yiseemcha Eloheem k'Efraim v'cheemenasseh

May God make you like Ephraim and Menasseh. (Genesis 48:20)

For girls, parents approach each daughter and gently place both their hands upon her head and recite:

Yesimech Eloheem k'Sarah, Rivka, Rachel v'Leah

May God make you like Sarah, Rebekah, Rachel and Leah.

For both boys and girls, conclude with the priestly blessing.

Yevarechecha Adonai v'yishmerecha
May God bless and keep you.

Ya'er Adonai panav eylecha veechuneka
May God's Presence shine and be good to you.

Yisa Adonai panav eylecha veyasem lecha shalom.
May God's face turn toward you and give you peace.

26
FASTING

And it shall be a statute for ever unto you: in the seventh month, on the tenth day of the month, you shall afflict your souls.

—Leviticus 16:29

DETAILS

The only fast day mentioned in the Torah is the Day of Atonement, Yom Kippur, described as a day of self-affliction. Traditionally understood, the command "you shall afflict your-selves" signifies abstinence from food. The Hebrew word *tzom* ("fasting") does not occur in the Five Books of Moses. The first mention of voluntary fasting is in connection with King David, who refused food when he prayed for the child borne to him by the wife of Uriah (II Samuel 12:22). At times, fasts were proclaimed because of calamity. The public fast meant that the people were conscious of guilt for which they humbled themselves before God. The fasting involved abstinence from iniquity and unlawful pleasures (Isaiah 58:3–10).

FASTING IN A NUTSHELL

The most well known and likely the most observed Jewish fast day is that of the Day of Atonement, Yom Kippur. It is a day of reflection and offering repentance to God. The fast on Yom Kippur begins at sundown on the eve of Yom Kippur and ends at nightfall the following day.

There are, however, other minor fasts on the Jewish calendar. For example, in the Book of Zechariah 8:19, four fasts are mentioned as occurring in the months of Tammuz (17th), Av (9th), Tishri (3rd), and Tevet (10th). They commemorate the Babylonian siege of Jerusalem on the tenth of Tevet (known in Hebrew as *asarah beTevet*), its capture on the seventeenth of Tammuz (in Hebrew, *shiv'ah asar beTammuz*), the destruction of the Temple on the ninth of Av (*tisha be'Av* in Hebrew), and the murder of Gedaliah and the Jews that were with him on the third of Tishri, called the fast of Gedaliah (*tzom Gedaliah* in Hebrew). These are fast days because tragic events happened on them.

Another fast, taking place on the eve of the Festival of Purim, is called the Fast of Esther (*ta'anit Esther* in Hebrew). This fast commemorates Esther's fast because before she went to plead with the king for her people she fasted for three days.

Unlike the fast of Yom Kippur and Tisha B'Av, which are observed from sunset to nightfall the following day, the fasting on all of the other fast days begins with daybreak and lasts till sunset, during which time food and drink of any kind is forbidden.

Judaism also has several other private noncommunal fasts. Here are several of the more well-known private fasts:

- On their wedding day, the bride and groom fast while repenting their past misdeeds. They ask forgiveness on the Day of Atonement.
- On the eve of Passover, there is a fast for firstborn sons in

memory of the deliverance of the Israelite firstborn, who were not stricken in Egypt with the tenth plague.

- There are some who fast on a Yahrzeit, the anniversary of a loved one's death.
- Special importance in Judaism has been attached to a fast resulting from a bad dream.

27

FORBIDDEN RELATIONSHIPS

None of you shall approach to any that is near of kin to him, to uncover their nakedness . . . I am God.

—Leviticus 18:6

The nakedness of your father and your mother, you shall not uncover.

—Leviticus 18:7

You shall not uncover the nakedness of your sister, the daughter of your father, or the daughter of your mother, whether born at home, or born abroad.

—Leviticus 18:9

You shall not uncover the nakedness of the daughter of your son or the daughter of your daughter.

—Leviticus 18:10

You shall not uncover the nakedness of the daughter of your father's wife, begotten of your father: she is your sister, and you shall not uncover her nakedness.

—Leviticus 18:11

You shall not uncover the nakedness of the sister of your father.

—Leviticus 18:12

You shall not uncover the nakedness of the sister of your mother.

—Leviticus 18:13

DETAILS

Various kinds of sexual control are found in almost all human societies. Among the most widespread of these is the prohibition of marriage and sex relations between blood relatives. The extent of these prohibitions varies, but everywhere sexual contact between parent and child is forbidden.

Biblical law forbids not only unions between close blood relatives but also, in certain instances, those between persons connected by marriage. Thus, one may not marry the widow of his father, uncle, or son.

Surprisingly missing from the list of forbidden relationships is that of the father and daughter. The ancient rabbis had to infer it from the prohibition of a union between grandfather and granddaughter.

FORBIDDEN RELATIONSHIPS IN A NUTSHELL

The Bible expressly forbade marriage and sex relations between blood relatives. Many commentators had different assertions related to these prohibitions. For instance, Maimonides argued that

69

sexual relations ought to be kept in moderation, and that it was scandalous for two blood relatives to have conjugal relations.

Nachmonides could not understand why sexual relations between relatives would be forbidden, since the Torah permitted a man to marry literally hundreds of wives. He guessed that perhaps it was not medically advisable for close relatives to have relations.

The passage about forbidden relations (Leviticus 18) is included as the Torah reading for the afternoon of Yom Kippur, the Day of Atonement. It was selected to impress upon people the need of maintaining Israel's high standard of chastity and family morality. Impurity in marriage, incestuous promiscuity among close relatives, and other abominations were condemned and regarded as unpardonable sins.

28
Four Species

And you shall take for yourselves on the first day the fruit of goodly trees, branches of palm trees and boughs of thick trees, and willows of the brook, and you shall rejoice before your God seven days.

—Leviticus 23:40

DETAILS

According to tradition, the four species specified in the biblical source cited above refer to the etrog (citron), the lulav (palm tree), the hadassim (twigs of myrtle), and the aravot (twigs of the willow tree). Rabbinic instruction states that the lulav, hadassim, and aravot are bound together and held by a person in his right hand, while the etrog is taken in the left. Holding both hands together, one says the blessings and waves the four species in all directions, as well as upward and downward. In this way one points to God's omnipresence.

FOUR SPECIES IN A NUTSHELL

The four species have been metaphorically interpreted by a variety of commentators throughout the centuries. The Hinnuch, for example, explains the commandment of taking the four species as follows: God commanded the Israelites to celebrate the joyous festival of Sukkot, at which time they would thank God for their bountiful harvest and rejoice during these festival days. Since joy very often evokes the physical, material self and can make a person forget one's reverence for God, God commanded the Israelites to take in their hands objects that would remind them that all of their rejoicing should be for the sake of God's glory. The etrog resembles the heart (the seat of a person's intelligence); the lulav is like a person's spine, reminding us that we must always stand erect when praying to God; the myrtle resembles eyes, implying that one should never go straying about following his eyes on the day of his heart's rejoicing; and the willow is like one's lips, which a person ought to hold in restraint, focusing solely on being in awe of God.

29
GOD'S THIRTEEN ATTRIBUTES

The Lord, the Lord is a merciful and gracious God, slow to anger and abounding in kindness and truth. God extended kindness to the thousandth generation, forgives iniquity, transgression and sin, and clears the guiltless.

—Exodus 34:6–7

DETAILS

The Bible distinguishes thirteen attributes of God listed in 34:67 of the Book of Exodus. Following is the way in which these attributes are rabbinically interpreted:

1. and 2. Adonai, Adonai: The Lord, the Lord. The traditional interpretation of the divine Name is that it discloses God's attribute of mercy. The repetition of the attribute of mercy was taken to mean that God is merciful both before and after man has sinned and repented. It is man who changes, not God.
3. *El* (God): "God," meaning His rulership, His being the Almighty.
4. *Rachum*: "Compassionate," sympathetic to suffering.

5. *Chanun*: "Gracious," in His helpful concern.

6. *Erech apayim*: "Slow to anger," giving human beings a chance to repent.

7. *Rav chesed*: "Abounding in kindness," beyond man's deserts.

8. *Emet*: "Truth," which in His case is here and elsewhere preceded by kindness.

9. *Notzer chesed la-alafim*: "Extending kindness to the thousandth generation," remembering human merit.

10., 11., and 12. *Nose avon vafesha ve-chata-ah*: "Forgiving iniquity, transgression and sin." God is indulgent with man's evil disposition (*avon*), his rebelliousness (*pesha*), and his guilt (*chata-ah*).

13. *Ve-nakeh lo yenakeh*: "Yet God does not remit all punishment." There are limits to God's mercy.

GOD'S THIRTEEN ATTRIBUTES IN A NUTSHELL

The thirteen attributes of God appearing in this biblical passage became a matter of intense discussion among Jewish scholars from the day of Philo on. They attempted to elicit from them comprehensive principles that would give people an insight into God's true being. Thus the philosopher Abraham ibn Daud deducted seven positive attributes: God's unity, truth, existence, omniscience, will, omnipotence, and being. The philosopher Maimonides claimed that these attributes only showed that God was ultimately unknowable. That is to say, we cannot know God in God's "positive" attributes (that is, what and how God is). According to Maimonides, the thirteen attributes interpret God's actions, not God's being. At best, we can only know what God is not (that is, God's "negative" attributes).

In modern times the philosopher Hermann Cohen condensed the thirteen attributes into two: love and justice.

These thirteen attributes are chanted aloud by the cantor during the service for taking out the Torah on Festivals that occur during the week.

30

HATRED

You shall not hate your brother in your heart.

—Leviticus 19:17

DETAILS

By and large, Judaism denounces hatred. "What is hateful to you, do not do to others," stated the rabbis (Talmud *Shabbat* 31a). The most vicious form of hatred, according to rabbinic tradition, is gratuitous hatred (*sinat hinnam*) or hatred without cause. This was considered hatred of the worst kind, and the rabbis always denounced it in extreme terms.

The emotion of anger can often lead one to hate another. A plethora of rabbinic statements related to anger, its control, and its potential hazards. Here are a sampling of them:

1. An angry person is unfit to pray. (Rabbi Nachman of Bratslav)
2. All the divisions of hell rule over the angry person. (Talmud *Nedarim* 22a)
3. Hillel used to say: "An angry person cannot be a teacher." (Ethics of the Fathers 2:6)
4. Do not grow angry and you will not sin. (Talmud *Berachot* 29)

76

HATRED IN A NUTSHELL

On November 4, 1995, Yitzhak Rabin, Prime Minister of Israel, was assassinated. Although scores of people of good will on all sides of the political issues have condemned the assassination, there remains a tide of extremist rhetoric and violence perpetuating the hatred that some people had for Rabin's attempt to make peace. The anger of the man who eventually killed Rabin was so out of control, and his hatred for him so deep, that he murdered the democratically elected leader of the State of Israel.

This is the kind of hatred that Judaism abhors. Gratuitous hatred—hatred without any real cause—was considered by the rabbis to be the most vicious form, and the ancient rabbis denounced it in extreme terms. To learn to subdue one's baser inclinations, a person was told to give priority to aiding the wicked rather than the good. Thus, the true object of proper hatred would be the actual sin and not the sinner, whose life must be respected and whose repentance must be effected.

The Ethics of the Fathers 2:15 sums up the rabbinic attitude toward hatred when it stated: "The hatred of other people destroys your own world."

31
HEAR O ISRAEL—SHEMA YISRAEL

Hear O Israel, the Lord is our God, the Lord is One. Love the Lord your God with all your heart, with all your soul, and with all your might. And these words which I command you this day you shall take to heart. You shall diligently teach them to your children. You shall recite them at home and away, morning and night. You shall bind them as a sign upon your hand, and they shall be a reminder above your eyes. You shall inscribe them on the doorposts of your homes and on your gates.

—Deuteronomy 6:4–9

DETAILS

Recited as the confession of the Jewish faith and belief in One God, the verse Shema Yisrael, Hear O Israel, sums up the first and second of the Ten Commandments. The Mishnah refers to the reciting of the Shema as the acceptance of the yoke of the divine majesty (Talmud *Berachot* 2:5). We are told that Rabbi Judah the Prince, when preoccupied with his studies, put his hand over his eyes and recited the first verse of the Shema in silence (Talmud *Berachot* 13b).

HEAR O ISRAEL—SHEMA YISRAEL— IN A NUTSHELL

The Shema Yisrael is Judaism's credo, proclaiming God's unity and uniqueness. It sums up Judaism's belief in monotheism and its rejection of idols. The Shema is also included in the mezuzah, which is affixed to the doorposts of Jewish homes, proclaiming their identity.

The Shema was also on the lips of the Jewish martyrs. Rabbi Akiba endured the greatest tortures while his flesh was being torn with iron combs and was said to have died pronouncing the last word *echad* (One) with his last breath. Indeed, the six words of the Shema have become the battle cry of the Jewish people for more than twenty-five centuries.

32
HELPING PEOPLE IN NEED

You shall not wrong a stranger or oppress him, for you were strangers in the land of Egypt. You shall not ill-treat any widow or orphan.

—Exodus 12:20–21

You shall not put a stumbling block in front of a blind person: You shall fear God.

—Leviticus 19:14

You shall not return a runaway slave to his master . . . Let him stay with you anywhere he chooses in any one of your settlements, whatever suits him best. You shall not wrong him.

—Deuteronomy 23:16–17

DETAILS

The Bible has always been cognizant of the plight of the poor, weak, and vulnerable. Among these are included the widow, the orphan, and the stranger. These are people who clearly are vulnerable and in need of a great deal of emotional support. In the case of widows and orphans, later Jewish law stipulates that financial support is not enough. They must be given emotional support as well.

Concerning the stranger, the Bible states that they are the sole category of people whom God is identified as loving. "And God loves the stranger" (Deuteronomy 10:18).

In an often quoted talmudic passage, Rabbi Eliezer comments on the surprising fact that the Bible demands no fewer than thirty-six times to love the stranger. The frequency of this repetition suggests that strangers had a difficult time and that instead of finding acceptance and friendship they often experienced rejection.

Since the Jewish people were strangers in so many foreign lands for hundreds of years, the Bible commanded them not to do to others what was done to them.

HELPING PEOPLE IN NEED IN A NUTSHELL

It is quite common in today's society for people to take advantage of society's weakest people. Among those in this category are placed the stranger, orphan, and widow—people who are often in need of an emotional and psychological lift. Because such people's spirits are often so very low, it is an obligation in Judaism to treat these people with unwavering courtesy and respect.

Some historians have noted that the long and historic Jewish involvement in human and civil rights is an outgrowth of the biblical reminder to Jews that they were strangers in the land of Egypt.

33

HOMOSEXUALITY

If a man lies with a male as one lies with a woman, the two of them have done an abhorrent thing. They shall be put to death—their bloodguilt is upon them.

—Leviticus 20:13

DETAILS

Homosexual conduct between males is mentioned much more frequently and more heavily condemned in the traditional Jewish sources than such conduct between females. The emphasis is on the sexual act between males rather than mental homosexual tendencies, as in Leviticus 19:22: "You shall not lie with mankind, as with womankind, both of them have committed abomination (Leviticus 20:13).

A debate dating from the second half of the second century is recorded in the Mishnah (Kiddushin 4:14). Rabbi Judah here forbids two unmarried males to sleep together, while the Sages permit it. The reason given (Kiddushin 82a) for the ruling of the Sages is that Jews are not suspected of engaging in homosexual practices. The Code of Jewish Law (Even Ha-Ezer 24), however, though recording the opinion of the Sages as the law, continues: "But in these times when there are many loose persons about, one should avoid being alone with another male."

Female homosexuality is referred to in the comment of the Sifra on the verse: "After the doings of the land of Egypt, wherein you dwelt, shall you not do. And after the doings of the land of Canaan, whither I bring you, shall you not do. Neither shall you walk in their statutes" (Leviticus 18:3). The Sifra observes that this does not mean that one must not copy the architectural styles, for instance, of Egypt and Canaan, but refers only to their sexual practices, in which they allowed men to marry men and women to marry women.

HOMOSEXUALITY IN A NUTSHELL

Traditional sources have shown that homosexual practices are severely frowned upon but female homosexuality is treated less severely than male homosexuality. Why this should be so is not stated in the sources but would appear to be due to the fact that in the nature of the case the possibility of physical contact is less than in the former instance. The sources also do not seem to recognize either male homosexuals or lesbians as distinct groups. In any event there is reference only to practices and not to some men or women having homosexual natures.

In recent years, Judaism's traditional rejection of homosexuality has come under attack. In 1972 the Reform branch of Judaism accepted a gay-oriented synagogue into the Union of American Hebrew Congregations. The Conservative and Reconstructionist Branches of Judaism are continuing to explore the issues of homosexuality, writing position papers.

34
HONESTY AND TRUTH

Keep far from falsehood.

—Exodus 23:7

DETAILS

Without truth and honesty, human society and human relationships cannot long endure. A customer making a purchase has to be able to trust the seller. A client has to believe his lawyer. Unless people tell each other the truth, our most basic relationships disintegrate.

It is therefore not surprising that Jewish tradition places great emphasis on the importance of telling the truth. The Torah says: "Keep far from falsehood" (Exodus 23:7). The Talmud (Pesachim 113b) puts it even more strongly when it says, "The Holy One hates a person who says one thing with his mouth and another in his heart."

HONESTY AND TRUTH IN A NUTSHELL

"The seal of the Holy Blessed One is truth" (Talmud *Shabbat* 55a). This rabbinic saying is most typical of the Jewish regard for truth. God is always to be found where there is truth. God's absence is felt where there is falsehood.

All of the Jewish moralists are eloquent in advocating truthfulness. For example, in Rabbi Isaac Aboab's *Menorat ha-Ma'or* (*Candelabrum of Light*), in the sections dealing with the virtue of truthfulness (Part II, 2:2), Aboab refers to the verses: "The Lord God is truth" (Jeremiah 10:10) and "Your Torah is truth" (Psalms 119:142). Telling lies to mislead others, says Aboab, is a serious offense, but even the telling of comparatively harmless lies is forbidden.

On the other hand, the rabbis believed that occasionally a "white lie" is permissible, for instance, when the intention is to promote peace and harmony (Talmud *Yevamot* 65b). The Talmud (Baba Metzia 23b–24a) observes that a scholar will never tell a lie except in the three instances of "tractate," "bed," and "hospitality." The commentators explain "tractate" to mean that a modest scholar is permitted to declare that he is unfamiliar with a tractate of the Mishnah in order not to flaunt his learning. "Bed" is understood to mean by the medieval commentator Rashi that if a man is asked intimate questions regarding his marital life he need not answer truthfully. Finally, "hospitality" is understood to mean that a man who has been generously treated by his host may decide not to tell the truth about his reception if he fears that as a result the host will be embarrassed by unwelcomed guests.

35
HONORING PARENTS

Honor your father and your mother, that you may long endure on the land that the Lord is assigning to you.

—Exodus 20:12

Honor your father and your mother, as the Lord your God has commanded you, that you may long endure, and that you may fare well, in the land that the Lord is assigning to you.

—Deuteronomy 5:16

A person should revere his [or her] mother and father.

—Leviticus 19:3

DETAILS

The religious obligation of honoring parents is taken directly from the fifth of the Ten Commandments. It is one of the few commandments in the Torah with a promise attached to it, namely length of days.

The ancient sages often refer to parents as God's co-partners in creation, hence the extreme care with which they must be respected by their children. The duty even extends beyond the grave: the memory of departed parents must be cherished in many ways.

According to Jewish law, the son is not to occupy his father's seat. He is not to contradict him or call him by his name. He can be compelled to maintain his parents. He must provide them with all their needs cheerfully. If he supports them with ill grace, he is said to incur divine punishment. He should under no circumstances insult them or display anger towards them. Though a daughter, too, is bound to honor her parents and do for them all she can, she is exempt from certain duties after her marriage, when she comes under her husband's authority and owes him devotion.

On the other hand, a parent is forbidden to be burdensome upon his children. He must not be too exacting. He should rather ignore their shortcomings and forgive them. A parent is forbidden to beat his grown son. The father especially exercises authority over the children during their minority, which ends with the boy at the beginning of the fourteenth year and with the girl at the beginning of the thirteenth. Anyone who beats his grown children is said to deserve excommunication, because in doing so he transgresses the divine commandment: "You shall not place an obstacle in front of the blind, but you shall revere your God" (Leviticus 19:14). A grown son, if enraged by his father, is likely to strike back.

HONORING PARENTS IN A NUTSHELL

Jewish tradition stresses the performance of good deeds and Torah study as the best method of honoring parents. When parents are upright, there is no limit to the reverence they deserve. Only a parent who leads an exemplary life and gives proper training to his children is entitled to respect and obedience.

Following are several rabbinic statements that provide an excellent summation to the Jewish attitude toward the honor to one's parents.

- When persons honor father and mother, God says, "I credit such action as if they had honored Me" (Talmud *Kiddushin* 30b).
- If you see your parents transgressing a mitzvah, do not say to them, "Father, Mother, you have disregarded a precept from the Torah." Rather, you should say, "Such-and-such is written in the Torah," speak to your mother and father as though you were consulting them instead of admonishing them (Mishneh Torah, Mamrim 6:11).
- "Honor your father and your mother just as you honor God, for all three have been partners in your creation (Zohar iii, 93a).
- Shimon bar Yochai said, "To honor one's parents is even more important than honoring God" (Jerusalem Talmud Peah, 15d).

36
HOSPITALITY

And God appeared to him [Abraham] by the terebinths of Mamre, as he sat in the tent door in the heat of the day. And he lifted his eyes and looked, and lo, three men stood over against him. When he saw them, he ran to meet them from the tent door, and bowed down to the earth. And he said: "My lord, if now I have found favor in your sight, pass not away, I pray you, from your servant. Let now a little water be fetched, and wash your feet and recline yourselves under the tree. And I will fetch a morsel of bread, and stay you your heart" . . . And Abraham hastened into the tent to Sarah, and said: "Make ready quickly three measures of fine meal, knead it, and make cakes." And Abraham ran to the herd, and fetched a calf tender and good, and gave it to the servant. And he hastened to dress it. And he took curd and milk, and the calf which he had dressed, and set it before them. And he stood by them under the tree, and they did eat.

—Genesis 18:1–8

DETAILS

The very strong feeling of hospitality among the Jewish people is reflected throughout the Bible and the Talmud. One of the Bible's earliest sources of hospitality is that of Abraham's hospitality and kindness to strangers in Genesis 18:1–8. The commentator the Ramban observes that although Abraham had many servants, he himself ran to the herd, because he was eager to show hospitality.

HOSPITALITY IN A NUTSHELL

Hospitality is generally regarded in contemporary circles to be no more than etiquette. However, in Jewish tradition, hospitality to guests and strangers (in Hebrew, *hachnasat orchim*) has been elevated to one of the essential religious obligations.

Throughout the history of the Jewish people, hospitality to guests has been a standard of proper Jewish manners. This mitzvah has developed into a means of showing personal and community concern for travelers and other guests. Warmly welcoming strangers and helping to satisfy their needs for food and lodging and for participation in religious celebrations grew to include friends and relatives, as well as travelers, to share in the joy of Sabbath and festival meals. Hosting a guest for the Sabbath or a festival became a sign of status in Jewish communities around the world. (This is especially true during Passover, which boasts of a seder meal that uses a Haggadah that opens with the statement of hospitality par excellence: "Let all who are hungry come and eat."

There are a whole host of rabbinic rules and advice vis-à-vis the responsibilities of a good host. They include the following:

1. Keeping an open house at all times. (See Ethics of the Fathers 1:5)

2. Displaying a flag to indicate mealtime. (See the Talmud *Baba Batra* 93b)
3. Providing choices of food when serving. (See Lamentations Rabbah 4:4)
4. Being cheerful at mealtime. (See Talmud *Derech Eretz Zuta* 9)
5. Having guests eat first. (See Talmud *Derech Eretz Zuta* 8)

37

JACOB'S LADDER

And he (Jacob) lighted upon the place, and tarried there all night, because the sun was set. And he took one of the stones of the place, and put it under his head, and lay down in that place to sleep. And he dreamed, and behold a ladder set up on the earth, and the top of it reached to heaven; and behold, the angels of God ascending and descending on it.

—Genesis 28:11–12

DETAILS

Jacob's ladder is the first explicitly recorded dream in the Bible. Ostensibly to find a wife from among his own kinsmen, but actually trying to escape the wrath of his twin brother Esau, Jacob set out for the land from whence his mother had come. Since travel after sunset became out of the question, Jacob lay down to spend the night under the open sky. There, on the road from Beersheba to Haran, he experienced an extraordinary dream vision that was eventually to prove a turning point in his life.

In this, Jacob's first encounter with God, fear and trembling is produced. Unlike in pagan mythology in which stairways often become passages of communication between humans and the gods,

Jacob's ladder does not serve this purpose. God does not descend the ladder nor does Jacob ascend it in an attempt to reach the divine realm. The ladder appears to be for the angels alone, whose purpose seems to be purely ornamental, rather than playing a role in Jacob's "vision" of God.

JACOB'S LADDER IN A NUTSHELL

Commentators have viewed the angels of God on Jacob's ladder with different interpretations. For instance, the Midrash Tanchuma holds that the angels were the princes of the heathen nations that God showed to Jacob. Jacob's dream thus depicted the rise and fall of nations and their cultures in the area of world history. Thus, according to the Midrash, the dream of Jacob was not understood as the dream of Jacob the individual, but rather of Jacob as the symbol of Israel. The angels symbolized the embodiment of the wanderings of the Jewish people, as they were exiled from one country to another, witnessing the rise and fall of mighty kingdoms such as Egypt, Assyria, and Babylon.

The rabbis of Midrash Rabbah (Genesis 28:12) related the entire Jacob episode of the ladder and the angels to the Mount Sinai experience. The ladder represented Mount Sinai, the angels of God alluded to Moses and Aaron. It is most interesting that in gematriah (Jewish numerology) both the Hebrew word for ladder (*sulam*) and the Hebrew word for Sinai (*seenai*) have the same numerical value of 130.

38
JUBILEE YEAR

You shall count seven sabbaths of years. And you shall hallow the fiftieth year and proclaim liberty throughout the land.

—Leviticus 25:8

DETAILS

The year of the jubilee (in Hebrew, *shnat hayovel*) resorts to the same principle as the sabbatical year. The fiftieth year, occurring after seven times seven years had been counted from the last jubilee, the land was to lie fallow, to show that it was not the absolute possession of man. Hence the law: "The land shall not be sold in perpetuity for the land is mine, and you are but strangers who have become my tenants" (Leviticus 25:23). Just like the Sabbatical year, the year of jubilee was designed to give the land a rest from agricultural work. Only the spontaneous produce of that year was to be enjoyed and shared with the poor and strangers.

JUBILEE YEAR IN A NUTSHELL

The Sabbatical year began with the first day of Tishri and the year of jubilee with the tenth of Tishri. In the Sabbatical Year, in addition to the land lying fallow, Hebrew slaves were to be set free if they desired their freedom and debts were to be remitted to Israelites. In the year of the jubilee, all property was to revert to the original owner who, through poverty, may have been obliged to sell it during the previous years. Hebrew slaves with their families were to be emancipated without price.

The fiftieth year was marked by the sounding of the ram's horn on the Day of Atonement, hence the Hebrew name "yovel," which means a ram's horn. The words "you shall proclaim liberty throughout the land," which appear in connection with the jubilee year, are inscribed on the Liberty Bell, which announced the signing of the United States Declaration of Independence.

Many commentators have asserted that the root meaning of the commandment of the jubilee year is that God desired to convey to His people that everything belongs to Him, and ultimately everything will return to whomever He gave it originally. By counting the years to the jubilee each year, people will be reminded that the earth belongs to God and they will be more likely to resist taking the land over their fellow brothers and sisters. The jubilee year also discourages those who view the land purely in terms of profit and protects those whose devotion to working the earth is rooted in love rather than greed.

39
JUSTICE

Judges and officers shall you make in all your gates, which the Lord your God gives you, tribe by tribe. They shall judge the people with righteous judgment. You shall not wrest judgment. You shall not respect persons. Neither shall you take a gift, for gift does blind the eyes of the wise and pervert the words of the righteous. Justice, justice, shall you follow, that you may live, and inherit the land which the Lord your God gives you.

—Deuteronomy 16:18–20

DETAILS

The repetition of the word *justice* in the last verse of the biblical source supports the view that the Jewish people had a passion for justice. In the Bible, the Hebrew root *tzdk*, generally translated in the sense of righteousness or justice, occurs over five hundred times, counting all its inflections. In the prophetic writings, justice is synonymous with ethical conduct. A person who refrains from wrongdoing and makes an effort to establish what is right is called just.

JUSTICE IN A NUTSHELL

The Bible, the Talmud, and the Codes of Jewish Law are a celebration of the demands of justice in human affairs. Abraham pleads with God himself to practice justice: "That be far from You to do after this manner, so slay the righteous with the wicked, that so the righteous should be as the wicked; that be far from You; shall not the judge of all the earth do justly?" (Genesis 18:25). In the Bible justice is demanded for the slave (Exodus 21:26–27), for the stranger (Exodus 22:20), for the widow and orphan (Exodus 22:21), for the poor (Exodus 22:24–26), even for animals (Exodus 22:29; Deuteronomy 22:6–7), and even for Israel's enemies (Deuteronomy 23:8–9).

The prophetic writings continually inculcate the need to practice justice. It is clear that Isaiah sees the good life in terms of justice (1:17-19): "Learn to do well—seek justice, relieve the oppressed, judge the fatherless, plead for the widow."

The minor prophet Micah's prescription has often been quoted as the highest demands of prophetic religion: "It has been told, O man what is good. And what God requires of you. Only to do justly, love mercy, and to walk humbly with our God" (Micah 6:8).

Based upon the biblical and rabbinic writings it is easy to understand why in modern times the Jewish people have been in the forefront of movements working for social justice, and why the biblical teachings have been the most powerful force for justice in the whole history of civilization.

40
LAW OF THE SHEKEL

And God spoke to Moses saying: "When you take the sum of the children of Israel, according to their number, then shall they give every man a ransom for his soul to God, when you number them. . . . This shall they give, every one that passes among them that are numbered, half a shekel after the shekel of the sanctuary. . . . Every one that passes among them that are numbered, from twenty years old and upward, shall give the offering of God. The rich shall not give more, and the poor shall not give less, than the half shekel, when they give the offering of the Lord.

—Exodus 30:11–15

DETAILS

Whenever a census of the warriors was taken, every adult Israelite was to pay a half-shekel. The money is described in the Bible as a "ransom for one's soul." This technical expression refers to the money paid by one who is guilty of taking human life in circumstances that do not constitute murder. Thus for example, the owner of the ox that had killed a man after the owner had received warning that the animal was dangerous was charged with the death of the man. But as his crime was not intentional, he was permitted to pay a ransom. This is the conception that underlies the biblical law of the half-shekel. The soldier who is ready to march into battle is in the eyes of God a potential taker of life though not a deliberate murderer. Thus he requires a ransom for his life.

LAW OF THE SHEKEL IN A NUTSHELL

Whether rich or poor, all souls are equal in the eyes of God. Thus, all were required to give the same ransom, namely one-half shekel.

In later years, the half-shekel became the annual tax devoted to maintaining the public services of the Temple. The daily worship was thus carried on by the entire people and not by the gifts of a few rich donors. The fact that only a half-shekel was paid taught that an individual's contribution to the community was only a fragment. For any complete work to be achieved on behalf of the sanctuary, the efforts of all, high and low, rich and poor alike, are required.

Today in modern times the memory of the half-shekel is still kept alive by the reading of Exodus 30:11–6 on the Sabbath before the Hebrew month of Adar (the month in which Purim falls) with a special Haftarah, Shekalim. Some also have the custom of donating half the value of a current silver coin to some worthy charitable cause on the festival of Purim.

41
LEPROSY

---

1. Leviticus 13:2–28, 38–39 (afflictions of the skin)
2. Leviticus 13:29–37 (afflictions of the hair)
3. Leviticus 13:45–46 (ostracism of the incurable)
4. Leviticus 14:1–32 (ritual for the rehabilitation of the healed leper)
5. Leviticus 14: 33–53 (diagnosis of the leprosy of houses)

DETAILS

Leprosy was the most dreaded disease in Bible times. It was believed that one was afflicted with it due to divine anger. The Hebrew term for leprosy *tzara'at* is not limited to true leprosy (Hansen's disease). It is rather a generic name, embracing a variety of skin ailments, including many noncontagious types. Thus, the leprosy of Miriam was transient (Numbers 12:10–15), and that of Naaman did not prevent him from mixing freely in society (II Kings 5).

LEPROSY IN A NUTSHELL

The debate continues as to whether the Hebrew word *tzara'at*, often translated as leprosy, ever means true leprosy. Medical commentators have variously suggested that it deals with eczema and psoriasis which are not contagious, of impetigo which is highly contagious, of gangrenous infections and true leprosy.

Regarding leprosy as a plague, the expression of God's anger, the Bible suggests that it may be brought about by several different sins and a variety of opinions on the subject appears in rabbinic writings. A favorite device of midrashic teachers was to pun on the Hebrew word *metzora*, "leper," and *motzi ra*, "slanderer." Thus, they utilized the reading of these Torah sections as an opportunity to preach against hostile talk and gossip.

The role of the priest vis-à-vis the leper was entirely ritualistic, and the priest never attempts to cure the leper. Indeed, the Bible says almost nothing about medical practice. The cures performed by Elijah and Elisha are presented as miracles.

42

Love Your Neighbor as Yourself

Love your neighbor as yourself.

—Leviticus 19:18

DETAILS

There is a well-known tale in the Talmudic tractate of *Shabbat* 31a. A man who wished to be converted to Judaism declared that he wished to be taught the whole of the Torah during the time he could stand on one leg. The teacher Shammai would have nothing to do with such an unreasonable request, but Hillel said to the man: "That which is hateful to you, do not do to your neighbor. This is the whole of the Torah. The rest is commentary. Go now and learn more about it."

It has been suggested that the Hebrew word *kamocha* (as yourself) does not refer to "you shall love" but "to your neighbor." The correct translation therefore would be: "love your neighbor who is yourself." The meaning is that we should treat our neighbors not as things to be used, but as persons like ourselves.

LOVE YOUR NEIGHBOR AS YOURSELF IN A NUTSHELL

The golden rule "love your neighbor as yourself" does not appear in the Book of Leviticus in isolation, but as part of a larger verse. The verse reads in full: "You shall not take vengeance, nor bear any grudge against the children of your people, but you shall love your neighbor as yourself: I am the Lord." Thus, the meaning of the verse in fact is that one ought not to practice revenge, and one ought not to try to get even with someone who has wronged another, but behave toward that person as if no wrong had been done.

The talmudic rabbis give these illustrations to define "taking revenge" and "bearing a grudge." If you ask someone to do you a favor and he refuses and later he asks you to do a favor which you refuse, you are taking revenge. If, on the other hand, when he asks you for a favor you do it, but recall that you are not acting like he did, you are not bearing a grudge. The point is that the verse is not thinking of feelings or emotions but of actions.

43

MANNA FROM HEAVEN

And when the layer of dew was gone up, behold upon the face of the wilderness was a fine, scale-like thing, fine as the hoar frost on the ground. And when the children of Israel saw it, they said to one another: "What is it?" for they knew not what it was. And Moses said to them: "It is the bread which the Lord has given you to eat."

—Exodus 16:14–15

DETAILS

About six weeks after the Israelites left Egypt, when they were not yet accustomed to life in the wilderness, the provisions that they had brought with them were exhausted. Soon after there appeared on the face of the wilderness a fine, scale-like thing. On seeing it, the Israelites asked one another: What is this? (In Hebrew, *man hoo*). They did not know what it was, but Moses explained to them that it was bread that God had given them to eat. It was like coriander seed, white, and had the taste of wafers made with honey.

The manna was miraculously supplied to the Israelites until they entered Canaan and the fruit of the land was available (Joshua 5:12).

MANNA FROM HEAVEN IN A NUTSHELL

According to talmudic tradition, many miracles occurred in connection with the daily descent of manna. No one could keep it for the next day or possess more than one omer, for it bred worms. Yet, the Sabbath portion, which came down in a double portion on Friday, remained fresh for the sacred day.

Some botanists have suggested that the extraordinary food the Israelites consumed in the wilderness for forty years which they called manna has a biological counterpart that exists naturally in the Sinai Peninsula. The substance was believed to be an exudation of the tamarisk, but it is now known to originate in an excretion of two scaled-insects that live in symbiosis with the tamarisk.

There are several major differences between the natural manna and the manna described in the Book of Exodus. The manna of today is relatively sparse and could not possibly provide enough food for the entire people of Israel. It is, of course, found on the Sabbath as well as on other days of the week. The biblical manna is clearly meant to be a food brought from heaven by God, interrupting the natural order by willing it so. It is meant to show God's care, concern, and love for His people. That is why manna has come to be known as "heavenly food," as it states in Psalm 105:40: "God satisfied them with food from heaven."

44

MEZUZAH

Inscribe them on the doorposts of your house and on your gates.

—Deuteronomy 6:9, 11:20

DETAILS

The Hebrew word for doorpost is *mezuzah*, and for centuries Jews have posted small boxes or receptacles known as *mezuzot* on their doorposts. Inside each box is a small scroll, which must be written by a scribe. The scroll's parchment contains the first and second paragraphs of the Shema, which includes the commandment concerning the *mezuzah*.

The word *Shaddai* (Almighty One) is written on the back of the parchment and is made visible through a small opening near the top of the case. According to Jewish law, every room in the house, except for the bathroom, should have a *mezuzah* on its doorpost. Interestingly, when a Jew moves into a new home, he or she is expected to put up a *mezuzah* immediately, or at least within the first thirty days. If the new family who is moving into the house is a Jewish one, the custom is to leave one's *mezuzot* for them.

MEZUZAH IN A NUTSHELL

The *mezuzah* serves as the distinctive mark of the Jewish home. It is fastened in a slanting position to the upper part of the doorpost on the right side of the entrance of each room, the upper end of the case pointing inward and the lower one outward. The attaching of the *mezuzah* to the doorpost is accompanied by the following special blessing:

Baruch atah Adonai elohaynu melech ha'olam asher kidshanu bemitzvotav vetzivanu likboah mezuzah.

Praised are You, Adonai our God, Sovereign of the Universe, who has made us holy with *mitzvot* and instructed us to affix the *mezuzah*.

Upon entering the house or leaving it, the custom is to touch the *mezuzah* with the fingers and then kiss the fingers. Rabbi Neil Gillman, quoting one of his students, has expressed a connection between speed bumps, which are built to slow cars down in public parking lots, and the *mezuzah*, which is a sort of speed bump. When a person enters or leaves a home and follows the custom of kissing the *mezuzah*, it allows just enough time for that person to slow down and always be reminded that the home one is entering or leaving is a sanctified one in which God is present.

45
MIKVEH

The Bible requires immersion in a mikveh *(ritual bath) to clean the body from impurity resulting from leprosy, discharge of semen, menstruation, childbirth, or contact with a corpse.*

—Leviticus 12:2, 15:5–13; Numbers 19:19

DETAILS

From ancient times until the present day, the *mikveh* has played a most important part in maintaining Jewish family purity. The water of the *mikveh* must come from a natural spring or river, and must be running, not drawn. The *mikveh* itself must have a minimum of 120 gallons of water.

Traditionally the *mikveh* is used by women after their menstrual cycle and in certain groups by both men and women as an aid to spirituality, particularly on the eve of the Sabbath and festivals, especially the Day of Atonement. Converts (Jews by choice) are required by Jewish law to use the *mikveh* as part of the ceremony of conversion.

The *mikveh* is also used in traditional settings to immerse new vessels and utensils manufactured by non-Jews (in accordance with Numbers 31:22–23).

MIKVEH IN A NUTSHELL

A *mikveh* is a ritual bath in which persons and utensils have to be immersed according to the laws of Judaism. Biblical law required the immersion in water to ritually purify oneself. Those who immersed included lepers, women after their menstrual cycle or childbirth, those who came into contact with the dead, and the high priest before officiating at the Yom Kippur services.

To be ritually fit for use, the *mikveh* must contain sufficient water to cover the body of a woman of average size. The water has to come from a natural spring or river.

Maimonides the philosopher and commentator stresses the symbolic significance of the *mikveh*, quoting from Ezekiel 36:25: "I will pour clean water over you to cleanse you from all your uncleanliness and from all of your idols."

46
MINYAN—QUORUM

How long shall I bear with this evil congregation that keep murmuring against me?

—Numbers 14:27

DETAILS

The number (*minyan*) of ten adult Jews is the minimum required for congregational worship, public Torah reading, the recitation of the Kedusha and Kaddish. The number ten for the minyan is said to have been derived from the Book of Numbers 14:27, where the ten spies (exclusive of Joshua and Caleb) are referred to in the verse as an *edah* (congregation). It has traditionally been deduced that a congregation for prayer must consist of at least ten male adults.

MINYAN—QUORUM—IN A NUTSHELL

The Mishnah *Megillah* 4:3 states: "If fewer than ten are present, the Shema and its accompanying blessings may not be recited with the reader who leads in the prescribed congregational prayers. Nor may the priestly benediction be pronounced by the kohanim, nor may the prescribed portions of the Torah and the Prophets be read . . . nor may the seven benedictions over the newly-wed be read . . . (*Megillah* 4:3).

Today the Reform, Conservative, and Reconstructionist branches of Judaism also include adult females in their count for a *minyan*. To show the equality of all adults in the make-up of a *minyan*, Rabbi Nachman of Bratslav said: "Nine righteous people do not make a *minyan*, but one common person, joining them, completes the *minyan*."

47

NOAH'S ARK

Then God said to Noah: "Go into the ark with all your household, for you alone have I found righteous before Me in this generation. Of every animal you shall take seven pairs, males and their mates, and of every animal that is not clean two, a male and its mate . . . For in seven days I will make it rain upon the earth, forty days and forty nights, and I will blot out from the earth all existence that I created." And Noah did as God commanded.

Noah was six-hundred years old when the Flood came, waters upon the earth. Noah, with his sons, wife, and his sons' wives, went into the ark because of the waters of the flood. . . .

The rain fell on the earth forty days and forty nights. . . . The waters swelled and increased greatly upon the earth, and the ark drifted upon the waters. When the waters had swelled much more upon the earth, all the highest mountains everywhere under the sky were covered. . . .

And when the waters had swelled on the earth one hundred and fifty days, God remembered Noah and all the beasts and all the cattle that were with him in the ark, and God caused a wind to blow across the earth, and the waters subsided. . . . At the end of one hundred and fifty days the waters diminished, so that in the seventh month, on the seventeenth day of the month, the ark came to rest on the mountains of Ararat.

At the end of forty days Noah opened the window of the ark that he had made and sent out the raven. It went to and fro until the waters had dried up from the earth. Then he sent out the dove to see whether the waters had deceased from the surface of the ground. But the dove could not find a resting place for its foot, and returned to him to the ark, for there was water over all the earth. . . . He waited another seven days, and again sent out the dove from the ark. The dove came back to him toward evening, and there in its bill was a plucked-off olive leaf. Then Noah knew that the waters had decreased on the earth. He waited still another seven days and sent the dove forth, and it did not return to him any more. . . .

So Noah came out, together with his sons, his wife and his sons' wives. Every animal, every creeping thing, and every bird, everything that stirs on earth came out of the ark by families . . .

—Genesis 7–9

DETAILS

Many diverse cultures tell stories about a great flood. Other cultures in the ancient Near East have their own stories related to an earth-wide catastrophe brought on by a deluge. Scientific investigation has attempted to show that sometime near the transition between prehistory and history, flood waters from the Persian Gulf may have covered the southern section of the Mesopotamian Valley. The many common elements in all these ancient Near Eastern flood stories and those of the Bible include the ark, the raven, and the dove. However, one fundamental difference between the biblical account and the others is that in the Bible it is human sin that raised God's anger to the point where God decided to put an end to the known world (with the exception of Noah, his family, and the animals).

Clearly, biblical man saw the hand of God in the flood, which was said to have lasted for 364 days, to indicate that the very cycle of nature was interrupted until heaven and earth returned to their shapes one year later. When the waters finally abated and Noah emerged from the ark, God pointed Noah to the special sign of a rainbow and stated that He would maintain a covenant with him and would never again destroy the entire world by a flood. God further said: "This is the sign that I set for the covenant between Me and you. . . . I have set My rainbow in the clouds, and it shall serve as a sign of the covenant between Me and the earth" (Genesis 9:12–13).

In ancient mythology, a rainbow represented instruments used by gods in battle. The bow would be suspended in the sky as a symbol of victory. The Hebrew word *keshet* means both "bow" and "rainbow."

NOAH'S ARK IN A NUTSHELL

During Noah's time the world had become permeated with violence and abhorrent behavior. God is grieved that He had created the world and decides to destroy the entire world by means of a flood. Only Noah and his family will be saved because Noah was righteous in his generation. Noah is told to build a huge ark and to put into it his family and pairs of animals too. God vows never again to destroy the world, and Noah and his family and the animals are saved.

The biblical story of Noah and the flood clearly demonstrates that all natural events and manifestations of the divine order are invested with divine portent. For the Israelites and Jewish people today, the sign of the rainbow is an eternal reminder of God's covenant of mercy. There is even a special blessing meant to be recited upon seeing a rainbow, which translates: "Praised are You, Adonai our God, Sovereign of the universe, who remembers His covenant, is faithful to it, and keeps His promise."

<h1 style="text-align:center">48</h1>

OBSERVING THE SABBATH

Remember the Sabbath day to keep it holy. Six days shall you labor, and do all your work. But on the seventh day is a sabbath to the Lord your God. In it you shall not do any manner of work, you, nor your son, nor your daughter, nor your man-servant, nor your maid-servant, nor your cattle, nor your stranger that is within your gates. For in six days God made heaven and earth, the sea, and all that is in them, and rested on the seventh day. Wherefore God blessed the Sabbath day and made it holy.

—Exodus 20:8–11

DETAILS

Already in biblical times, the Sabbath was singled out as the most important of all the Jewish festivals. It was the only one included in the Ten Commandments. In obeying the commandment to desist from working on the Sabbath and making it a day of rest and renewal, the Israelites in a sense were following the pattern of God's creative labor. God fashioned the heavens and the earth and all the living creatures, and then God rested. Linked with the creation, the Sabbath has been regarded as a perpetual sign between

God and the people of Israel, symbolizing the duty of work and the holiness of rest.

OBSERVING THE SABBATH IN A NUTSHELL

The traditional predominant feature of the Sabbath is cessation from labor and business activity. The Sabbath was designed to raise a person's life to a higher level by affording him or her a day of rest and imparting the idea of human equality. Thus the common epithet applied to the Sabbath is holy.

Almost all of the aspects of the Sabbath are summed up in the blessing over the wine (the Kiddush) recited in the homes and also in the synagogues on Friday nights: "You have sanctified us with your commandments . . . you have graciously given us Your holy Sabbath as a heritage, in remembrance of the creation."

Many beautiful home customs have arisen in connection with Sabbath observance. Three festive Sabbath meals are a religious duty, often accompanied by the singing of Sabbath songs. Family blessings, blessings over the Sabbath *hallah*, and the grace after the meal are also part of the Sabbath traditional protocol.

Perhaps no statement more aptly sums up the importance of the Sabbath to the Jewish people than this statement by the philosopher Ahad Ha'Am: "More than Israel has kept the Sabbath, it is the Sabbath that has kept Israel."

49
PEACE

May God lift His countenance upon you and give you peace.

—Numbers 6:27

DETAILS

The Hebrew word *shalom*, used as a greeting or farewell, can be best translated as completeness or wholeness. Although often translated as peace, it signifies welfare of every kind: contentment, security, prosperity, friendship, and tranquility of mind. A peace-pursuing person is held in highest esteem in Judaism. In fact, the person who loves and pursues peace is regarded as a disciple of Aaron, the High Priest.

PEACE IN A NUTSHELL

The three-fold priestly blessing concludes with a statement asking that God grant a person peace. When Jewish tradition speaks of peace, it does not mean merely an absence of strife. Rather, peace implies a striving for harmony and unity among people.

Hillel once said: "Love peace and strive for peace" (Ethics of

118

the Fathers 1:12). Among talmudic statements about peace the following may be quoted: "The whole Torah exists only for the sake of peace. For the sake of peace, truth may be sacrificed" (Talmud *Gittin* 59b; *Yevamot* 65b).

The traditional Jewish greeting when one person meets another is "shalom aleichem"—"peace be with you." And a well-known verse in Psalm 34:14 says "seek peace and pursue it." The Bible does not obligate the Jewish people to pursue the mitzvot, but only to fulfill them at the proper time, at the appropriate occasion. Peace, however, must be sought at all times: at home and away from home Jews are obliged to seek peace and pursue it (Midrash, Numbers Rabbah 19:27).

50
PIDYON HABEN—
REDEMPTION OF THE FIRSTBORN

The first issue of the womb of every being, man or beast, that is offered to God, shall be yours; but you shall have the first born of man redeemed. . . . Take as their redemption price from the age of one month up, the money equivalent of five shekels by the sanctuary weight.

—Numbers 18:15–17

DETAILS

The Jewish people had special rites and responsibilities for its firstborn. Jews consecrated their firstborn, endowing them with leadership and special responsibilities. For example, the firstborn Israelite son received the birthright, which made him the head of the entire family clan and the owner of the family's material possession.

When the Jewish people started their wanderings in the desert after having worshiped the golden calf, the situation vis-à-vis firstborns changed. A tabernacle was built in the wilderness, and the special duties of the firstborn were transferred to the Levites, a priestly tribe. The Bible then decreed that every father release his firstborn son from his special duties by redeeming him from a *Kohen*. Since that time Jews follow the custom of releasing the firstborn male child of his ancient obligation with a ceremony called a *pidyon haben*, meaning "redemption of the firstborn son."

PIDYON HABEN—REDEMPTION OF THE FIRSTBORN—IN A NUTSHELL

The Bible states that a child from a month old shall be redeemed. From this statement the rabbis deduced that a *pidyon haben* takes place after the first month of life, or thirty days after birth. Since Jews have always found it desirable to observe a religious ordinance as soon as possible, the *pidyon haben* generally takes place on the thirty-first day after birth. If the thirty-first day falls on a Sabbath or Festival, the redemption is postponed until the following day.

Jewish law requires that a *pidyon haben* be performed if the child is male and the first issue of the womb. If the child's father is a *kohen* or a Levite, that child automatically belongs to the special caste of ministers called Kohanim and Leviim and need not have a *pidyon haben*. Also, if the mother of the child is the daughter of a *kohen* or Levi, the rite is not performed. Finally, a male child born by Caesarean section does not have to be redeemed, because Jewish law does not consider such a child as "issuing forth" from the womb.

In order to conduct a *pidyon haben* ceremony one needs a cup of wine, a challah (part of the festive meal to follow), a *kohen*, the firstborn male son and his parents, five shekels (silver dollars are often used today), and the officiant (usually the rabbi or cantor or a knowledgeable Jewish layperson).

The father hands over his son to the *kohen* and gives the *kohen* five silver dollars. The *kohen* receives the redemption money and returns the child to his father whereupon the father recites: "Praised are You, God, who made us holy with Your *mitzvot* and commanded us concerning the redemption of the firstborn."

51

PROCREATION

Be fruitful and multiply, and fill the earth and subdue it.

—Genesis 1:28

DETAILS

To "be fruitful and multiply" is one of Judaism's most important commandments. It has rabbinically been interpreted to mean that a man must beget at least two children—a son and a daughter to fulfill this commandment. According to rabbinic tradition, when a man reaches the age of eighteen, he becomes subject to the commandment to marry and have children.

PROCREATION IN A NUTSHELL

The Jewish people are a people of the family and that is why it is a religious obligation in Judaism for one to get married and have children. According to the commentator called the Hinnuch, the purpose of the commandment of procreation is that God's desire to have the world inhabited with people be fulfilled. For only with a world of people can God expect to have His commandments fulfilled.

52
PROHIBITED WORK

The seventh day is a sabbath unto God. In it you shall do no manner of work, you, nor your son, nor your daughter, nor your man servant, nor your maid-servant, nor your cattle, nor your stranger that is within your gates.

—Exodus 20:9–10

You shall keep the sabbath therefore, for it is holy to you; every one that profanes it shall surely be put to death; for whosoever does any work therein, that soul shall be cut off from among his people.

—Exodus 31:14

DETAILS

Linked with the creation of the world, the Sabbath has been regarded as a perpetual sign between God and the people of Israel, symbolizing the duty of work and the holiness of rest. The Bible commands: "Six days you shall labor and do all your work, but on the seventh day, which is a Sabbath in honor of God, you shall not do any work (Exodus 29:9–10).

Work, or *melacha* which is the Bible's term for it, is rabbinically interpreted to mean thirty-nine categories of work that were conducted during Temple times and forbidden on the Sabbath. The thirty-nine categories are:

1. Ploughing
2. Sowing
3. Reaping
4. Sheaf-making
5. Threshing
6. Winnowing
7. Selecting
8. Sifting
9. Grinding
10. Kneading
11. Baking
12. Sheep-shearing
13. Bleaching
14. Combing raw materials
15. Dyeing
16. Spinning
17., 18., 19. Weaving operations
20. Separating into threads
21. Tying a knot
22. Untying a knot
23. Sewing
24. Tearing
25. Trapping or hunting
26. Slaughtering
27. Skinning
28. Tanning
29. Scraping pelts
30. Marking out

31. Cutting to shape
32. Writing
33. Erasing
34. Building
35. Demolishing
36. Kindling a fire
37. Extinguishing
38. Kindling a fire
39. Carrying from the private to the public domain or vice versa

PROHIBITED WORK IN A NUTSHELL

The main source in the Bible for the definition of Sabbath work is the command that all of the various activities necessary for the construction of the tabernacle in the wilderness should cease on the Sabbath (Exodus 31:13). All of these are expressly included in the Hebrew term *melacha*, which rabbinically has been interpreted to include thirty-nine forbidden categories of activity. When one carefully examines the list of forbidden categories, one sees that it forms a cross section of all the main types of human productive activity.

In arriving at his interpretation of *melacha*, the commentator Samson Raphael Hirsch starts with the basic idea that the Sabbath testifies to God as the Supreme Creator of heaven and earth and all they contain. Man, however, is engaged in a constant struggle to gain mastery over God's creation, to bring nature under his control. By the use of his God-given intelligence and skill, man has in large measure succeeded in doing this. He is thus in constant danger of forgetting about his dependence upon God for all things. To recognize God as Creator of all, the Bible has thus commanded man to refrain from working on one day a week, the holy Sabbath.

By doing this, man proclaims God as the Source of all power. Thus one definition of a *melacha* would be an act that shows man's mastery of the world by the constructive use of his intelligence and skill.

53

PROHIBITION AGAINST INTERMARRIAGE

You shall not intermarry with them; do not give your daughters to their sons or take their daughters for your sons.

—Deuteronomy 7:3

DETAILS

Marrying within Judaism has always been encouraged among Israelites. In one of the earliest Bible stories, Abraham instructs his servant Eliezer to find a wife for his son Isaac from his own family. By the time of Ezra (400 B.C.E.), intermarriages were deemed socially and politically so undesirable that they had to be dissolved.

PROHIBITION AGAINST INTERMARRIAGE IN A NUTSHELL

Judaism stresses the importance of marrying within the faith and preserving its heritage of culture and traditions. Examples in the Bible abound on the subject of opposition to mixed marriage. Isaac charges his son Jacob not to take a wife from among the Canaanites, a non-Israelite people inhabiting ancient Palestine (Genesis

28:1). There is extreme bitterness of Isaac and his wife Rebekah when they learn that their son Esau has taken Hittite wives (Genesis 26:34–35). In the strongest of all biblical denunciation of mixed marriages, Ezra orders all intermarried Jews to divorce their Gentile wives (Ezra 9:12).

Aside from the important consideration of marital harmony, Judaism opposes mixed marriage because it poses a threat to the future of the Jewish people and to their faith, customs, and traditions. As a minority, the Jewish people seek to preserve their Jewish identity and find it crucial to resist the inroads of mixed marriage.

54

REBELLIOUS SON

If a man has a wayward and defiant son, who does not listen to his father or mother and does not obey them even after they discipline him, his father and mother shall take hold of him and bring him out to the elders of the town at the public place of his community. They shall say to the elders of the town, "This son of ours is disloyal and defiant. He does not listen to us. He is a glutton and a drunkard." Thereupon the men of his town shall stone him to death. Thus you will sweep out evil from your midst. All Israel will hear and be afraid.

—Deuteronomy 21:18–20

DETAILS

The severe punishment of an incorrigible son described in the Book of Deuteronomy was never administered, according to a talmudic statement in the tractate *Sanhedrin* 71a. The biblical law merely stresses the community's interest in the proper upbringing of children. When the authority of the parents is powerless, that of the state must be exercised.

The Mishnah (*Sanhedrin* 8:4) enumerates several conditions upon which the condemnation of the rebellious son depends: "If his father was willing to accuse him but his mother was not, or if his father was not willing but his mother was, he cannot be condemned as a stubborn and rebellious son. . . . If his parents were not compatible, he cannot be condemned. . . . If either of them was maimed in hand or lame or dumb or blind or deaf, he cannot be condemned. . . . They must warn him, and scourge him before three judges. If he again behaves in an evil manner, he must be tried before twenty-three judges. He may only be stoned if the first three judges are there."

REBELLIOUS SON IN A NUTSHELL

The law of a rebellious son applies to one beyond the age of thirteen years and one day, exhibiting signs of puberty, when he already possesses a mind of his own but is still under the control of his parents who are without defect so that they can fully exercise their authority under normal conditions. When the entire blame cannot be placed on the son because of disagreement between his parents who are not fit for each other, he is left unpunished. Thus, the Talmud says that the law of a rebellious son, which can never be carried out on account of the numerous strictures, was imposed merely for the purpose of receiving a reward through studying it.

55

REQUIREMENT OF TWO WITNESSES

Whoever kills a person, the murder shall be slain at the mouth of two witnesses, but one witness shall not testify against any person that he die.

—Numbers 35:30

DETAILS

This commandment refers to the requirement of two witnesses to testify in the case where a death sentence is involved. Qualifications of witnesses were of utmost importance, since most trials were based completely upon the testimony of eyewitnesses. Among those rabbinically excluded in giving testimony in capital cases were women, minors, professional gamblers, and all of those who knowingly transgressed the laws of the Torah or were ignorant of them.

REQUIREMENT OF TWO WITNESSES IN A NUTSHELL

The Bible demands at least two witnesses in trials involving the possibility of capital punishment. Circumstantial evidence of the most conclusive kind was not admitted in the Jewish superior courts of the twenty-three judges having jurisdiction in capital crimes. There was no torture of the accused to compel confession, since this would not be in keeping with an essential principle of Jewish law according to which "no person can by his own testimony incriminate himself in a capital charge" (Talmud *Sanhedrin* 9b).

If the testimony given by the witnesses was found to agree, the presiding judge began by encouraging the prisoner to refute it by producing contradictory witnesses. He also appealed to the members of the court to advance arguments in favor of the prisoner.

Abrabanel suggests that since one man is on trial, it logically follows that more than one witness is needed to prove his guilt. If there was need of only one witness, then the case would be one person's word against another.

56

REVERENCE FOR THE AGED

You shall rise before the aged and show deference to the old. You shall fear your God.

—Leviticus 19:32

Ask your father and he will tell you, your elders and they shall instruct you.

—Deuteronomy 32:7

DETAILS

The above biblical source (Leviticus 19:32) is posted in Israeli buses to encourage people to offer their seats to the elderly. The rabbis understood the biblical source from Leviticus 19:32 quite literally—that whenever an old person passes by one should rise to one's feet as a token of respect. The Talmud (*Kiddushin* 33a) states that the third-century Palestinian teacher Rabbi Yochanan would rise to his feet even when heathens who were old passed by because, he said, they have had so many troubles in their long life. Jewish tradition has always been sensitive to the needs of the elderly. Older adults were held in high esteem in the Bible and in rabbinic tradition. There was always the recognition that the wisdom accrued through life's experience would be extremely valuable to the leadership of the community. Throughout Jewish history, the elders were sought for advice because they had participated in so many of life's experiences. We read in the Ethics of the Fathers (4:28) this verse: "A person who learns from the young may be compared to one who eats unripe grapes and drinks wine from a vat, but a person who learns from the old may be compared to one who eats ripe grapes and drinks wine that is aged."

RESPECT FOR THE AGED IN A NUTSHELL

It was Rabbi Nachman of Bratzlav who once said that the prosperity of a country is in accordance with the treatment of its aged. The Jewish community has always valued and respected the elderly. When the aged needed support to live independently and the family lacked the necessary resources, the Jewish community provided assistance. The first Jewish home for the aged in the United States was established in St. Louis in 1855. During the next century and a half to follow, most cities with large Jewish communities established Jewish homes for the elderly. Today, many synagogues and Jewish Community Centers have special programs for older adults, providing them with opportunities to study, to create, and to grow as human beings and as members of the Jewish community with a great deal to contribute.

The whole philosophy of care for the aged is expressed in the Psalmist's poignant cry (Psalms 71:9) "Cast me not off in the time of old age. When my strength fails, do not forsake me."

Respect for the aged became a dominant idea and was expressed in daily Jewish life. Perhaps this verse from Psalm 92:14 sums up the value of the elderly throughout their life: "In old age they shall still produce fruit, they shall be full of vigor and strength."

57

THE RIGHTEOUS WAY TO GIVE—
TZEDAKAH

When you reap the harvest of your land, do not reap the edges of your field. Also, do not gather the gleanings of your harvest. Do not pick your vineyard bare or gather its fallen fruit. Leave them for the poor and for the stranger. I am Adonai, your God.

—Leviticus 19:9–10

Open your hand to the poor and your neighbors in your land who are in need.

—Deuteronomy 15:11

You shall surely tithe all the increase of your seed.

—Deuteronomy 14:22

DETAILS

The Hebrew word for charity is *tzedakah*. It is derived from the Hebrew word *tzedek*, which means "righteous" or "just." Thus tzedakah for the Jewish people is the righteous way to give.

136

According to the Talmud, tzedakah is required of all people, rich and poor. No matter where one is in life, there are always people less fortunate.

Here are several rabbinic statements related to tzedakah:

- "Be generous in giving tzedakah, but beware of giving all that you have." (Talmud *Arachin* 28a).
- "Even a poor person who lives on tzedakah should practice tzedakah" (Talmud *Gittin* 7a).
- "The blessing of tzedakah is greater for the person who gives than the person who receives" (Leviticus Rabbah 34:10).
- "The person who gives only a little honestly earned money to tzedakah is better than the person who gives lots of money that has been gained through fraud" (Ecclesiastes Rabbah 4).
- "The ultimate purpose of the laws of tzedakah is to nurture in people the quality of mercy and kindness and not just eliminate poverty. God could have accomplished that by providing for the needs of the poor without human intervention" (Sefer Hahinnuch 66, Parashat Mishpatim).
- "Rabbi Hillel used to say: The more tzedakah, the more *shalom*" (Ethics of the Fathers 2:8).

THE RIGHTEOUS WAY TO GIVE— TZEDAKAH—IN A NUTSHELL

The Bible and the rabbinic codes emphasize the need to care for the poor. Every Jewish community has had an organized system of relief for the poor, the members being taxed for this purpose. In addition, private donors gave of their wealth to assist the poor.

The Jewish ideals of tzedakah were summarized and taught by

Moses Maimonides, the great teacher and philosopher who lived eight-hundred years ago in Spain and then Egypt. Maimonides believed that tzedakah is like a ladder with eight rungs from bottom to top. Each step you climb brings you closer to Heaven:

1. The person who gives reluctantly and with regret.
2. The person who gives graciously, but less than one should.
3. The person who gives what one should, but only after being asked.
4. The person who gives before being asked.
5. The person who gives without knowing to whom he or she gives, although the recipient knows the identity of the donor.
6. The person who gives without making his or her identity known.
7. The person who gives without knowing to whom he or she gives. The recipient does not know from whom he or she receives.
8. The person who helps another to become self-supporting by a gift or a loan or by finding employment for the recipient.

58

RIGHTS OF A WIFE

If he takes for himself another wife, her food, clothing and conjugal rights shall he not diminish.

—Exodus 21:10

DETAILS

It was a husband's biblical obligation to his wife to supply her with food and clothing and to have sexual relations with her. During biblical times in which men ruled supreme and societies were patriarchal, this law was very important in that it offered important protection to a woman, helping to serve her basic needs.

RIGHTS OF A WIFE IN A NUTSHELL

There are six rabbinic obligations that relate to a husband's obligation toward his wife. They include the following:

- To fulfill the obligations of the *ketubah* (Jewish marriage contract) in which there is a monetary settlement when a husband divorces his wife.
- To pay for her medical care.
- To ransom her if she is captured.

- To give her a dignified burial.
- To make provisions to support her with his assets should he die prior to her death.
- To provide for the support of their unmarried daughter after his death.
- To make provisions that if his wife should die before him, the sons that she bore him will inherit any property she brought with her as her marriage portion.

59

ROSH HASHANAH AND SOUNDING THE RAM'S HORN

In the seventh month, on the first day of the month, you shall observe complete rest, a sacred occasion with loud blasts. You shall not work at your occupations.

—Leviticus 23:24–25

DETAILS

This biblical prescription refers to the commemoration of the festival of Rosh Hashanah, which today ushers in the new Jewish year. Rosh Hashanah, which means "head of the year," marks the beginning of the Jewish calendar. It falls on the first and second days of the month of Tishri, the seventh month of the Jewish calendar. Many years ago, the Jewish people had several dates in the calendar marking the beginning of important seasons of the year. The first month was Nisan, in the spring, when the Jewish people were freed from Egyptian slavery. The first of Tishri was the beginning of the economic year, the time when the old harvest ended and the new one began. In time, the first of Tishri became the beginning of the year.

ROSH HASHANAH AND SOUNDING THE RAM'S HORN IN A NUTSHELL

Leviticus 23:24–25 describes one of the oldest instruments called a *shofar* (ram's horn), which was sounded to announce the beginning of the new year. In modern times during the Rosh Hashanah service, blasts of the shofar are sounded at various intervals during the morning service. It is a commandment to hear the sounding of the shofar.

The *shofar* is a reminder for people to awaken and repent. It has also served as a reminder of the ram that Abraham sacrificed in place of his own son Isaac. The story of the binding of Isaac is the Bible reading on the festival of Rosh Hashanah.

60
Sabbatical Year

Six years you shall sow your land and gather its yield. But in the seventh you shall let it rest and lie fallow. Let the needy among your people eat of it, and what they leave let the wild beasts eat.

—Exodus 23:10–11

DETAILS

Plowing, planting, and reaping are the essential labors that have kept people alive since the beginning of time. Yet once every seven years, God commands the Israelites to put away the spade and hoe, relinquish all control of the fields and orchards, and let the earth lie fallow. This year of rest is known in Hebrew as *shnat hashemittah*, the year of relaxation during which the land was to lie fallow and be withdrawn from cultivation.

The laws of the Sabbatical Year apply only to Jews who live in the land of Israel.

SABBATICAL YEAR IN A NUTSHELL

Although the majority of Israeli Jews do not adhere to the strict standards of this religious obligation, the Sabbatical Year establishes an important principle. It represents the first recorded agricultural dictum that allows the land and soil to replenish itself by lying fallow for a year. Furthermore, it offers to the underprivileged an opportunity to receive the fruits of the Sabbatical Year.

Many commentators have offered their rationales for the creation of the Sabbatical Year. In the explanation of Ibn Ezra, he parallels the plan of God with that of humankind. Just as God rested on the seventh day from His creation, so too humans are commanded to rest the soil. For Ibn Ezra, each year is the equivalent of one day of creation.

Maimonides presents the scientific explanation for the Sabbatical Year, stating that allowing the land to lie fallow gives it an opportunity to rejuvenate itself and yield more abundant crops in the years to come.

Finally, the Keli Yakar states that the law of the Sabbatical Year presents people with their opportunity to show faith in God. That is to say, one must certainly have faith that God will provide adequate crops in every sixth year if one is commanded to let his land lie fallow in the seventh.

61
SACRIFICES

*Cain brought of the fruit of the ground. Abel brought of the
firstlings of his flock and of the fat thereof.*

—Genesis 4:3–4

*If his offering be a burnt offering of the herd, he shall offer
it a male without blemish.*

—Leviticus 1:3

*And when the days of her purification are fulfilled, for a
son, or for a daughter, she shall bring a lamb of the first
year for a burnt offering, and a young pigeon or a turtle
dove, for a sin offering, to the door of the tent of meeting,
unto the priest.*

—Leviticus 12:6

*When he shall be guilty in one of these things, he shall confess
regarding that which he transgressed. And he shall bring
his forfeit to God for his sin which he has sinned, a female
from the flock, a lamb or a she-goat, for a sin offering, and
the priest shall make atonement for him as concerning his
sin.*

—Leviticus 5:5–6

And you shall offer one he-goat for a sin offering, and two male lambs of the first year for a sacrifice of peace offerings. And the priest shall wave them with the bread of the first fruits for a wave offering before the Lord, with the two lambs.

—Leviticus 23: 19–20

If he offer it for a thanksgiving, then he shall offer with the sacrifice of thanksgiving unleavened cake mingled with oil, and unleavened wafers spread with oil, and cakes mingled with oil, of fine soaked flour. With cakes of leavened bread he shall present his offering with the sacrifice of his peace offerings for thanksgiving.

—Leviticus 7:12–13

And you shall put the whole upon the hands of Aaron, and upon the hands of his sons. And you shall wave them for a wave offering before God.

—Exodus 29:24

DETAILS

The Hebrew word *korban* (sacrifice) meaning literally "to bring near" or "to approach" occurs some eighty times in the Bible, especially in the books of Leviticus and Numbers. A sacrifice was, therefore, a means to approach God. From the dawn of human history, the sacrificial offering was the basis of divine worship. They

146

were generally offered to obtain God's favor and to atone for the sins of the sacrificer.

The first sacrifices recorded in the Bible were offered in Genesis 4:4 by Cain ("fruit of the soil") and Abel ("the choicest of the firstborn of his flock"). Noah made an offering (Genesis 8:20) that the Bible describes as having a pleasant odor. Sacrifices were also made at various local shrines, such as Beth-el, Shiloh, and Hebron.

Although the libation of wine and meal offerings played a prominent role in some of the rituals, the most important biblical sacrifices were animals. The sacrificial animal has to be wholly unblemished, domesticated, and the property of the person making the sacrifice.

SACRIFICES IN A NUTSHELL

The sacrifices can be divided into various categories: propitiatory and dedicatory offerings, meal offerings, libation offerings, fellowship offerings, thanksgiving offerings, free-will offerings, and ordination offerings.

Propitiatory Offerings

Two offerings belong to this category: the sin offering, called "chattat," and the guilt offering, called "asham." The sin offering was suited to the rank and the circumstance of the person who offered it. Thus, the High Priest would bring a young bull (Leviticus 4:3), a nasi ("ruler") would bring a male goat (Leviticus 4:23), and a commoner would bring a female goat (Leviticus 4:28) or a lamb (Leviticus 4:32). A sin offering of one male goat was required on each of the sacred festivals: the New Moon (Numbers 28:15), each day of Passover (Numbers 25:22–24), Shavuot

(Numbers 28:30), Rosh Hashanah (Numbers 29:5), Yom Kippur (Numbers 29:11), and each day of Sukkot (Numbers 29:16, 19).

The guilt offering was a special kind of sin offering (Leviticus 5:7) that was required when someone was found to have been denied his or her rightful due. The guilty party had to bring an offering, usually in the form of a ram.

Burnt Offerings

An olah, from the Hebrew word meaning "to go up," used the following animals: bulls, sheep or goats, and birds (Leviticus 1:3–17). A continual burnt offering, called an "olah tamid," was made twice daily during biblical times. It consisted of two male lambs that were sacrificed, one in the morning and one in the evening (Exodus 29:38–42). Two additional lambs were offered each Sabbath (Numbers 28:9–10).

Various purification rituals also called for burnt offerings: childbirth (Leviticus 12:6–8), unclean issues (Leviticus 15:14–15), and hemorrhages (Leviticus 15:29–30).

Meal Offerings

Regularly accompanying the animal sacrifices was the meal offering (*mincha*, in Hebrew). The meal offering generally consisted of a mixture of fine flour, oil, and frankincense, and often took the form of baked loaves or wafers. The meal offering usually accompanied each burnt offering, and its quantity was generally fixed according to the animal being sacrificed. Meal offerings were rendered after such joyous occasions as the cleansing of a leper (Leviticus 14:10) and the successful consumption of a Nazirite vow (Numbers 6:15). No meal offering accompanied the rite of cleansing after childbirth or unclean issues.

Libation Offerings

The libation (*nesech* in Hebrew) normally accompanied both the burnt offering and the peace offering (Numbers 15:1–10). The libation, a drink offering of wine, was considered an additional "pleasing odor" offering (Numbers 15:7), and the amount of wine used depended upon the type of animal being sacrificed. Libation offerings were mentioned in the Bible in connection with the Sabbath (Numbers 28:9), the New Moon (Numbers 28:14), Shavuot (Numbers 29:18), and Passover (Numbers 28:16–29).

Peace Offerings

Called *shelamim* in Hebrew, the peace offering was the basic sacrifice of all communal sacrifices. Any domesticated animal was permitted for use as a peace offering, which always concluded with some type of communal meal. The peace offering was specified for only the celebration of Shavuot (Leviticus 23:19–20), the ritual for the completion of a Nazirite vow (Numbers 6:17–20), and the installation of priests (Exodus 29:19–34).

Thanksgiving Offering

Known in Hebrew as *zevach*, this is the most frequently mentioned type of peace offering (Leviticus 7:12–13).

Wave Offering

Known in Hebrew as a *tenufah*, the priest's portion of the peace offering was "waved" before God, an act that demonstrated that the offering belonged to God. The waving was only a preliminary to offering up the animal or meal offering on the altar fire (Exodus 29:24, 26).

Free Will Offering

Called a *nedavah*, this was the minimum offering that could be brought to the holy convocations that took place on the Three Pilgrimage Festivals. It could be burnt in addition to a peace offering (Leviticus 22:17–24).

62

SACRIFICE OF ISAAC

And it came to pass after these things that God did prove Abraham, and said unto him: "Abraham"; and he said: "Here am I." And God said: "Take now your son, your only son, whom you love, even Isaac, and get you into the land of Moriah. And offer him there for a burnt offering upon one of the mountains of which I will tell you." And Abraham rose early in the morning and saddled his donkey and took two of his young men with him, and his son Isaac, and he cleaved the wood for the burnt offering, and rose up, and went to the place of which God had told him. On the third day Abraham lifted up his eyes and saw the place from afar. And Abraham said to his young men: "Abide here with the donkey, and I and the lad will go yonder. And we will worship and come back to you." And Abraham took the wood for the burnt offering, and laid it upon Isaac his son, and he took in his hand the fire and the knife. And they went both of them together. And Isaac spoke to Abraham his father, and said: "My father." and he said: "Here am I, my son." And he said: "Behold the fire and the wood, but where is the lamb for the burnt offering?" And Abraham said:

"God will provide Himself the lamb for a burnt offering, my son." So they went both of them together. And they came to the place which God had told him, and Abraham built the altar there and laid the wood in order, and bound his son Isaac, and laid him on the altar, upon the wood. And Abraham stretched forth his hand, and took the knife to slay his son. And the angel of God called to him out of heaven, and said: "Abraham, Abraham." And he said: "Here am I." And he said: "Lay not your hand upon the lad, neither do anything to him. For now I know that you are a God-fearing man, seeing you have not withheld your son, your only son, from Me." And Abraham lifted up his eyes, and looked, and beheld him a ram caught in the thicket by his horns. And Abraham went and took the ram, and offered him up for a burnt offering in the stead of his son. And Abraham called the name of that place Adonai Yireh, as it is said to this day: "In the mount where God is seen." And the angel of God called to Abraham a second time out of heaven, and said: "By Myself have I sworn, says God, because you have done this thing, and have not withheld your son, your only son, that in blessing I will bless you, and in multiplying I will multiply your seed as the stars of the heaven, and as the sand which is upon the sea-shore. And your seed shall possess the gate of his enemies. And in your seed shall all the nations of the earth be blessed. Because you have listened to My voice." So Abraham

returned to his young men, and they rose up and went together to Beer-sheba, and Abraham dwelt at Beer-sheba.

—Genesis 22:1–19

DETAILS

The Hebrew term *akedah*, "binding," signifies the attempted sacrifice of Isaac by his father Abraham, whose faith was put to the ultimate test when he was commanded to present his beloved son Isaac as a burnt offering on one of the mountains in the land of Moriah. According to rabbinic tradition, this was the tenth and the greatest of the trials Abraham had to face, to prove that he was worthy of being the founding father of the Jewish people. The narrative concerning the binding of Isaac also portrays the faith and obedience of the second Jewish patriarch, Isaac. The willingness of Abraham and the readiness of Isaac are symbolic of supreme trust and devotion of Jewish martyrdom followed by divine mercy. For this reason the story of the binding of the Isaac is frequently recalled in the liturgy. The sounding of the shofar, the ram's horn, on Rosh Hashanah serves as a reminder of the horn of the ram that was sacrificed by Abraham in place of Isaac.

SACRIFICE OF ISAAC IN A NUTSHELL

Few chapters of the Bible have had a more lasting influence upon Israel than Genesis, chapter 22. When the angel of the Lord forbade Abraham to slay his son Isaac, a ram that was caught in the thickets was substituted as a sacrifice. At a time when the cruel heathen deities demanded the sacrifice of their children to the gods, Judaism taught that the God of Abraham strictly forbids human

153

sacrifice. Abraham was now assured that because he had stood the test, a great future was in store for his offspring.

The theme of the binding of Isaac is expressed in several prayers in the High Holy Day liturgy, intending to arouse God's compassion for Isaac's descendants and to inspire people to deeds of sacrifice.

Abraham's willingness to sacrifice his greatest possession on the altar of his God evoked a new ideal in Israel, the ideal of martyrdom. As persecution against the Jew increased, the story of the binding of Isaac gave the Jewish people the courage to prefer death to apostasy.

63

SANCTIFICATION OF THE NEW MOON

This month shall be for you your beginning of months. It shall be for you the first month of the year.

—Exodus 12:2

DETAILS

Unlike the secular (Gregorian) calendar, which is solar, the Jewish calendar is both lunar and solar. The months are fixed by the moon's movements around the earth, the years by the earth's revolution around the sun. Since the lunar year (354 days) is shorter than the solar year (365 days), a system was devised to coordinate the lunar with the solar year. The method that was adopted utilizes the periodic addition of a "leap month" to make the years more equal in length and ensure that the Jewish festivals always occur at the correct season.

In ancient times, the determination of the lunar month was facilitated by two eyewitnesses sent by the Jewish Court to look for the new moon. When the court was convinced that their determination was satisfactory, the *Bet Din* (Jewish Court) proclaimed that day to be the new month. The announcement of the new moon was done by signaling from hilltop to hilltop, using small fires. The use of the ram's horn was also used to signal the new month.

SANCTIFICATION OF THE NEW MOON IN A NUTSHELL

In the middle of the fourth century of the common era, Hillel II published scientific rules for the computation of the calendar, making it possible to determine the Jewish calendar without actual observation of the lunar phases. According to this system, the months alternate between thirty and twenty-nine days. When the preceding month has thirty days, its last day is celebrated as the first day of Rosh Hodesh, while the second day of Rosh Hodesh marks the first day of the new month.

Today, the new month is observed in synagogues on the first day of every month in the Hebrew calendar. Hallel psalms of praise are recited during the morning service, and the scriptural Torah reading for Rosh Hodesh (Numbers 28:1–5) describes the special sacrificial offerings for each new month in biblical times.

The day preceding Rosh Hodesh has been, since the sixteenth century, identified as Yom Kippur Katan (Minor Day of Atonement), devoted to repentance and penitential prayers recited after the Mincha afternoon service. Some observe the custom of fasting on this day, a custom said to have been inaugurated in circles close to Rabbi Isaac Luria, the famous mystic of Safed.

64

SAVING A LIFE—PIKUACH NEFESH

You shall, therefore, keep My statutes and My ordinances,
which if a man do he shall live by them.

—Leviticus 18:5

DETAILS

The duty of saving an endangered life suspends the operation of all the religious obligations in the Torah, with the exception of three prohibitions: no person is to save his life at the price of murder, adultery, or idolatry. The sages of the Talmud interpret the words "he shall live by them" in Leviticus 18:5 to mean that the mitzvot, the divine commands, are to be a means of life and not of death. Specifically, the duty of saving a life supersedes even the laws of the Sabbath. The humanitarian definition of the suspension rule signifies the duty to promote life and health. From a Jewish point of view, it is sinful to observe laws that are in suspense on account of the danger to life or health. One may do any work on the Sabbath to save a life (Talmud *Ketubot* 5a). "The Sabbath has been given to you, not you to the Sabbath" is a well-known statement in the Talmud (*Yoma* 85b).

SAVING A LIFE—PIKUACH NEFESH— IN A NUTSHELL

The rationale for violating Jewish laws when life is at stake is based on verse 5 in the eighteenth chapter of the Book of Leviticus which states: "You shall, therefore, keep My statutes and My ordinances, which if a man do he shall live by them." The rabbis understood this to mean "You shall live by them, and not die by them" (Talmud *Yoma* 85b).

In his *Mishneh Torah*, Maimonides the philosopher discusses the duty of profaning the Sabbath when failure to do so is certain to endanger human life:

> The commandment of the Sabbath, like all other commandments, are set aside if human life is in danger. Accordingly, if a person is dangerously ill, whatever a skilled local physician considers necessary may be done for him on the Sabbath. (*Mishneh Torah*, Laws of the Sabbath 2:2)

As previously mentioned, the only exceptions to the law of saving a life and violating a Jewish law are in the instances of murder, idolatry, and forbidden sexual relations. The laws related to saving a life reflect the premium that Judaism assigns to human life.

65

SEVEN NOACHIAN PRECEPTS

God blessed Noah and his sons and said to them: "Be fruitful and multiply, and replenish the earth. . . . Only flesh with the life thereof, of which is the blood thereof, shall you not eat. Whosoever sheds man's blood, by man shall his blood be shed." For in the image of God He made man. . . . And God said to Noah: "This is the token of the covenant which I have established between Me and all flesh that is upon the earth."

—Genesis 9:1, 4, 17

DETAILS

The term *Noachians* (the sons of Noah) denotes all of the descendants of Noah who survived the flood along with his closest kin. The seven precepts of Noah, distinct from the laws obligatory on the Israelites alone, are binding on all human beings. They prohibit idolatry, murder, theft, blasphemy, incest, eating the flesh of a live animal, and they include the duty of promotion of justice. All non-Jews who observe these laws, upon which all civilized society depends, are deemed worthy of life in the world to come.

SEVEN NOACHIAN PRECEPTS IN A NUTSHELL

By observing these seven Noachian precepts as a minimum, a non-Jew settling among Jews might enjoy the privileges and responsibilities of a full-fledged proselyte. Thus there is no imperative need for a non-Jew to adopt the Jewish faith to merit salvation.

The attitude of Judaism to conversions is based on the conception of the seven precepts imposed on the descendants of Noah or the entire human species. The Noachian precepts represent a theory of universal religion, emphasizing good actions rather than right belief, ethical living rather than credal adherence. They require only loyalty to a basic code of ethical conduct and rest upon the recognition of a divine Creator.

66

THE SIX HUNDRED THIRTEEN COMMANDMENTS

POSITIVE COMMANDMENTS

The Jew is required to (Exod. 20:2) believe that God exists and (Deut. 6:4) acknowledge God's unity; to (Deut. 6:13) love, (Deut. 6:13) fear, and (Exod. 23:25) serve God. The Jew is also instructed to (Deut. 10:20) cleave to God (by associating and imitating the wise) and to (Deut. 19:20) swear only by God's name. One must (Deut. 28:9) imitate God and (Lev. 22:32) sanctify God's name.

The Jew must (Deut. 6:7) recite the *Shema* each morning and evening and (Deut. 6:7) study the Torah and teach it to others. The Jew should bind *tefillin* on (Deut. 6:8) head and (Deut. 6:8) arm. The Jew should make (Num. 15:38) *tzizit* for the garments and (Deut 6:9) fix a *mezuzah* on the door. The people are to be (Deut. 31:12) assembled every seventh year to hear the Torah read and (Deut. 17:18) the king must write a special copy of the Torah for himself. (Deut. 31:19) Every Jew is to have a Torah scroll. One must (Deut. 8:10) praise God after eating.

The Jews are to (Exod. 25:8) build a Temple and (Lev. 19:30) respect it. It must be (Num. 18:4) guarded at all times, and (Num. 18:23) the Levites are to perform their special duties in it. Before entering the Temple or participating in its service, the priests (Exod. 30:19) must wash their hands and feet; they must also (Exod. 27:21) light the candelabrum daily. The priests are required to (Num. 6:23) bless Israel and (Exod. 25:30) set the shewbread and frankincense before the Ark. Twice daily they must (Exod. 30:7) burn the incense on the golden altar. (Lev. 6:6) Fire shall be kept burning on the altar continually and the ashes must be (Lev. 6:3) removed daily. Ritually unclean persons must be (Num. 5:4) kept out of the Temple. Israel (Lev. 21:8) is to honor its priests, who must be (Exod. 28:2) dressed in special priestly raiment. The priests are to (Num. 7:9) carry the Ark on their shoulders, and (Exod. 30:31) the holy annointing oil must be prepared according to its special formula. (Deut. 18:6–8) The priestly families are to officiate in rotation. In honor of certain dead close relatives the priests must (Lev. 21:2–3) make themselves ritually unclean. The high priest may marry (Lev. 21:13) only a virgin.

The (Num. 28:3) *tamid* sacrifice must be offered twice daily, and the (Lev. 6:13) high priest must also offer a meal-offering twice daily. An additional sacrifice (*musaf*) must be offered (Num. 28:9) every Sabbath, (Num. 28:11) on the first of every month, and (Lev. 23:26) on each of the seven days of Passover. On the second day of Passover (Lev. 23:10) a meal offering of the first barley must also be brought. On Shavuot a (Num. 28:26–27) *musaf* must be offered and (Lev. 23:17) two loaves of bread as a wave-offering. The additional sacrifice must also be made on (Num. 29:1–2) Rosh Hashanah and (Num. 28:26–27) on the Day of Atonement when the (Lev. 16) *Avodah* must also be performed. On every day of the festival of (Num. 29:13) Sukkot a *musaf* must be brought, as well as on the (Num. 29:36) eighth day thereof.

Every male [and female] Jew is to make (Exod. 23:14) pilgrimage to the Temple three times a year and (Exod. 34:23) appear there during the three pilgrim Festivals. One must (Deut. 16:14) rejoice on the festivals.

On the fourteenth of Nisan one must (Exod. 12:6) slaughter the paschal lamb, and one must (Exod. 12:8) eat of its roasted flesh on the night of the fifteenth. Those who were ritually impure in Nisan are to slaughter the paschal lamb on the (Num. 9:11) fourteenth of Iyar and eat it with (Num. 9:11, Exod. 12:8) *matzah* and bitter herbs. Trumpets should be (Num. 10:10; 10:9) sounded when the festive sacrifices are brought and also in times of tribulation.

Cattle to be sacrificed must be (Lev. 22:27) at least eight days old and (Lev. 22:21) without blemish. All offerings must be (Lev. 2:13) salted. It is a *mitzvah* to perform the ritual of (Lev. 1:2) the burnt-offering, (Lev. 6:18) the sin-offering, (Lev. 7:1) the guilt-offering, (Lev. 3:1) the peace-offering, and (Lev. 2:1, 6:7) the meal-offering.

Should the Sanhedrin err in a decision its members (Lev. 4:13) must bring a sin-offering, which offering must also be brought (Lev. 4:27) by a person who has unwittingly transgressed a *karet* prohibition [that is, an act that incurs *karet* if done deliberately]. When in doubt as to whether one has transgressed such a prohibition, a (Lev. 5:17–18) "suspensive" guilt-offering must be brought.

For (Lev. 5:15, 21–25; 19:20–21) stealing or swearing falsely and for other sins of a like nature, a guilt-offering must be brought. In special circumstances the sin-offering (Lev. 5:1–11) can be according to one's means.

One must (Num. 5:6–7) confess one's sins before God and repent for them.

A (Lev. 15:13–15) man or (Lev. 15:28–29) woman who has a seminal issue must bring sacrifice; a woman must also bring a sacrifice (Lev. 12:6) after childbirth.

A leper must (Lev. 14:10) bring a sacrifice after he [or she] has been cleansed.

One must (Lev. 27:32) tithe one's cattle. The (Exod. 13:2) firstborn of clean [that is, permitted] cattle are holy and must be sacrificed. Firstborn sons must be (Exod. 22:28; Num. 18:15) redeemed. The firstling of the ass must be (Exod. 34:20) redeemed; if not (Exod. 13:13) its neck has to be broken.

Animals set aside as offerings (Deut. 12:5) must be brought to Jerusalem without delay and (Deut. 12:14) may be sacrified only in the Temple. Offerings from outside the land of Israel (Deut. 12:26) may also be brought to the Temple.

Sanctified animals (Deut. 12:15) that have become blemished must be redeemed. A beast exchanged for an offering (Lev. 27:33) is also holy.

The priests must eat (Lev. 8:9) the remainder of the meal-offering and (Exod. 29:33) the flesh of sin-and-guilt offerings; but consecrated flesh that has become (Lev. 7:19) ritually unclean or (Lev. 7:17) that was not eaten within its appointed time must be burned.

A Nazirite must (Num. 6:5) let his hair grow during the period of his separation. When that period is over he must (Num. 6:18) shave his head and bring his sacrifice.

A person must (Deut. 23:24) honor his vows and oaths which a judge can (Num. 30:3) annul only in accordance with the law.

Anyone who touches (Lev. 11:8, 24) a carcass or (Lev. 11:29–31) one of the eight species of reptiles becomes ritually unclean; food becomes unclean by (Lev. 11:34) coming into contact with a ritually unclean object. Menstruous women (Lev. 15:19) and those lying-in after childbirth (Lev. 12:2) are ritually impure. A leper (Lev. 13:3), (Lev. 13:51) a leprous garment (Lev. 13:51), and a leprous house (Lev. 14:44) are all ritually unclean. A man having a (Lev. 15:2) running issue is unclean, as is (Lev. 15:16) semen. A woman suffering from (Lev. 15:19) a running issue is also impure. A human corpse (Num. 19:14) is ritually unclean. The purification water (*mei niddah*) purifies (Num. 19:13, 21) the unclean, but it makes the clean ritually impure. It is a mitzvah to become ritually clean (Lev. 15:16) by ritual immersion. To become cleansed of leprosy one (Lev. 14:2) must follow the specified procedure and also (Lev. 14:9) shave off all of one's hair. Until cleansed the leper (Lev. 13:45) must be bareheaded with clothing in disarray so as to be easily distinguishable.

The ashes of (Num. 19:2–9) the red heifer are to be used in the process of ritual purification.

If a person (Lev. 27:2–8) undertakes to give his [or her] own value to the Temple, he [or she] must do so. Should a person declare an unclean beast (Lev. 27:11–12), a house (Lev. 27:14), or a field (Lev. 27:16, 22–23) as a donation to the Temple, he must give their value in money as fixed by the priest. If one unwittingly derives benefit from Temple property (Lev. 5:16), full resitution plus a fifth must be made.

The fruit of (Lev. 19:24) the fourth year's growth of trees is holy and may be eaten only in Jerusalem. When you reap your fields you must leave the corners (Lev. 19:9), the gleanings (Lev. 19:9), the forgotten sheaves (Deut. 24:19), the misformed bunches of grapes (Lev. 19:10), and the gleanings of the grapes (Lev. 19:10) for the poor.

The first fruits must be (Exod. 23:19) separated and brought to the Temple, and you must also (Deut. 18:4) separate the great heave-offering (*terumah*) and give it to the priests. You must give (Lev. 27:30; Num. 18:24) one tithe of your produce to the Levites and separate (Deut. 14:22) a second tithe, which is to be eaten only in Jerusalem. The Levites (Num. 18:26) must give a tenth of their tithe to the priests.

In the third and sixth years of the seven-year cycle you must (Deut. 14:28) separate a tithe for the poor instead of a second tithe. A declaration (Deut. 26:13) must be recited when separating the various tithes and (Deut. 26:5) when bringing the first fruits to the Temple. The first portion of the (Num. 15:20) dough must be given to the priest.

In the seventh year (*shemittah*) everything that grows is (Exod. 23:11) ownerless and available to all; the fields (Exod. 34:21) must lie fallow and you may not till the ground. You must (Lev. 25:10) sanctify the Jubilee [fiftieth] year, and on the Day of Atonement in that year (Lev. 25:9) you must sound the *shofar* and set all Hebrew slaves free. In the Jubilee year all land is to be (Lev. 25:24) returned to its ancestral owners; and generally, in a walled city (Lev. 25:29–30) the seller has the right to buy back a house within a year of the sale.

Starting from entry into the land of Israel, the years of the Jubilee must be (Lev. 25:8) counted and announced yearly and septennially.

In the seventh year (Deut. 15:3) all debts are annulled, but (Deut. 15:3) one may exact a debt owed by a foreigner.

When you slaughter an animal you must (Deut. 18:3) give the priest his share as you must also give him (Deut. 18:4) the first of the fleece. When a person makes a *cherem* [special vow], you must (Lev. 27:21, 28) distinguish between what belongs to the Temple [that is, when God's name is mentioned in the vow] and between what goes to the priests. To be fit for consumption, beast and fowl must be (Deut. 12:21) slaughtered according to the law, and if they are not of a domesticated species (Lev. 17:13) their blood must be covered with earth after the slaughtering.

Set the parent bird (Deut. 22:7) free when taking the nest. Examine beast (Lev. 11:2), fowl (Deut. 14:11), locusts (Lev. 11:21), and fish (Lev. 11:9) to determine whether they are permitted for consumption.

The Sanhedrin is to (Exod. 12:2, Deut. 16:1) sanctify the first day of every month and reckon the years and the seasons.

You must (Exod. 23:12) rest on the Sabbath day and (Exod. 20:8) declare it holy at its onset and termination. On the fourteenth of Nisan (Exod. 12:15) remove all leaven from your ownership, and on the night of the fifteenth (Exod. 13:8) relate the story of the Exodus from Egypt; on that night (Exod. 12:8) you must also eat matzah. On the (Exod. 12:16) first and (Exod. 12:16) seventh days of Passover you must rest. Starting from the first day of the first sheaf [the sixteenth of Nisan] you shall (Lev. 23:35) count forty-nine days. You must rest on (Lev. 23) Shavuot and on (Lev. 23:24) Rosh Hashanah; on the Day of Atonement you must (Lev. 16:29) fast and (Lev. 16:29, 31) rest. You must also rest on (Lev. 23:35) the first and (Lev. 23:42) the eighth day of Sukkot, during which festival you shall (Lev. 23:42) dwell in booths and (Lev. 23:40) take the four species. On Rosh Hashanah (Num. 29:1) you are to hear the sound of the *shofar*.

Every male is to (Exod. 30:12–13) give half a shekel to the Temple annually. You must (Deut. 18:15) obey a prophet and (Deut. 17:15) appoint a king. You must also (Deut. 17:11) obey the Sanhedrin; in the case of division, (Exod. 23:2) yield to the majority. Judges and officials shall be (Deut. 16:18) appointed in every town and they shall judge the people (Lev. 19:15) impartially.

Whoever is aware of evidence (Lev. 5:1) must come to court to testify. Witnesses shall be (Deut. 13:15) examined thoroughly and, if found to be false, (Deut. 19:19) shall have done to them what they intended to do to the accused.

When a person is found murdered and the murderer is unknown, the ritual of (Deut. 21:4) decapitating the heifer must be performed.

Six cities of refuge are to be (Deut. 19:3) established. The Levites, who have no ancestral share in the land, shall (Num. 35:2) be given cities to live in.

You must (Deut. 22:8) build a fence around your roof and remove potential hazards from your home.

Idolatry and its appurtenances (Deut. 12:2, 7:5) must be destroyed, and a city which has become perverted must be (Deut. 13:17) treated according to the law. You are instructed to (Deut. 20:17) destroy the seven Canaanite nations, and (Deut. 25:19) blot out the memory of Amalek, and (Deut. 25:17) to remember what they did to Israel.

The regulations for wars other than those commanded in the Torah (Deut. 20:11–12) are to be observed, and a priest must be (Deut. 20:2) appointed for special duties in times of war. The military camp must be (Deut. 23:14–15) kept in a sanitary condition. To this end, every soldier must be (Deut. 23:14) equipped with the necessary implements.

Stolen property must be (Lev. 5:23) restored to its owner. Give (Deut. 15:8; Lev. 25:35–36) charity to the poor. When a Hebrew slave goes free the owner must (Deut. 15:14) give him gifts. Lend to (Exod. 22:24) the poor without interest; to the foreigner you may (Deut. 23:21) lend at interest. Restore (Deut. 24:13; Exod. 22:25) a pledge to its owner if he needs it. Pay the worker his wages (Deut. 24:15) on time; (Deut. 23:25–26) permit him to eat of the produce with which he is working. You must (Exod. 23:5) help unload an animal when necessary, and also (Deut. 22:4) help load human or beast [of burden]. Lost property (Deut. 22:1; Exod. 23:4) must be restored to its owner. You are required (Lev. 19:17) to reprove the sinner, but you must (Lev. 19:18) love your neighbor as yourself. You are instructed (Deut. 10:19) to love the proselyte. Your weights and measures (Lev. 19:36) must be accurate.

Respect the (Lev. 19:32) wise; (Exod. 20:12) honor and (Lev. 19:3) revere your parents. You must (Gen 1:28) perpetuate the human species by marrying (Deut. 24:1) according to the law. A bridegroom is to (Deut. 24:5) rejoice with his bride for one year. Male children must (Gen. 17:10; Lev. 12:3) be circumcised. Should a man die childless, his brother must either (Deut. 25:5) marry his widow or (Deut. 25:9) release her (*chalitza*). He who violates a virgin must (Deut. 22:29) marry her and may never divorce her. If a man unjustly accuses his wife of premarital promiscuity (Deut. 22:18–19), he shall be flogged and may never divorce her. The seducer (Exod. 22:15–23) must be punished according to the law. The female captive must be (Deut. 21:11) treated in accordance with her special regulations. Divorce can be executed (Deut. 24:1) only by means of a written document (*get*). A woman suspected of adultery (Num. 5:15–27) has to submit to the required test.

When required by the law, (Deut. 25:2) you must administer

the punishment of flogging and you must (Num. 35:25) exile the unwitting homicide. Capital punishment shall be by (Exod. 21:20) the sword, (Exod. 21:16) strangulation, (Lev. 20:14) fire, or (Deut. 22:24) stoning, as specified. In some cases the body of the executed (Deut. 21:22) shall be hanged, but it (Deut. 21:23) must be brought to burial the same day.

Hebrew slaves (Exod. 21:2) must be treated according to the special laws for them. The master is to (Exod. 21:8) marry his Hebrew maidservant or (Exod. 21:8) redeem her. The alien slave (Lev. 25:46) must be treated according to the regulations applying to him.

The applicable law must be administered in the case of injury caused by (Exod. 21:18) a person, (Exod. 21:28) an animal, or (Exod. 21:33–34) a pit. Thieves (Exod. 21:37) must be punished. You must render judgment in cases of (Exod. 22:4) trespass by cattle, (Exod. 22:5) arson, (Exod. 22:6–8) embezzlement by an unpaid guardian, and in claims against (Exod. 22:9–12) a paid guardian, a hirer, or (Exod. 22:13) a borrower. Judgment must also be rendered in disputes arising out of (Lev. 25:14) sales, (Exod. 22:8) inheritance and (Deut. 25:12) other matters generally. You are required to (Num. 27:8) rescue the persecuted even if it means killing the oppressor.

PROHIBITIONS

It is (Exod. 20:3) forbidden to believe in the existence of any but the One God.

You may not make images (Exod. 20:4) for yourself or (Lev. 19:4) for others to worship or for (Exod. 20:20) any other purpose.

You must not worship anything but God either in (Exod. 20:5) the manner prescribed for Divine worship or (Exod. 20:5) in its own manner of worship.

Do not (Lev. 18:21) sacrifice children to Molech.

You may not (Lev. 19:31) practice necromancy or (Lev. 19:31) resort to familiar spirits; neither should you take idolatry or its mythology (Lev. 19:4) seriously.

It is forbidden to construct a (Deut. 16:21) pillar or (Lev. 20:1) dias even for the worship of God or to (Deut. 16:21) plant trees in the Temple.

You may not (Exod. 23:13) swear by idols or instigate an idolator to do so, nor may you encourage or persuade any (Exod. 23:13) non-Jew or (Deut. 13:12) Jew to worship idols.

You must not (Deut 13:9) listen to or love anyone who disseminates idolatry, nor (Deut. 13:9) should you withhold yourself from hating him [or her]. Do not (Deut. 13:9) pity such a person. If somebody tries to convert you to idolatry (Deut. 13:9), do not defend that person or (Deut. 13:9) conceal the fact.

It is forbidden to (Deut. 7:25) derive any benefit from the ornaments of idols. You may not (Deut. 13:17) rebuild what has been destroyed as a punishment for idolatry, nor may you (Deut. 13:18) gain any benefit from its wealth. Do not (Deut. 7:26) use anything connected with idols or idolatry.

It is forbidden (Deut. 18:20) to prophesy in the name of idols or prophesy (Deut. 18:20) falsely in the name of God. Do not (Deut. 13:3–4) listen to the one who prophesies for idols, and do not (Deut. 18:22) fear the false prophet or hinder his execution.

You must not (Lev. 20:23) imitate the ways of idolaters or practice their customs; (Lev. 19:26; Deut. 18:10) divination, (Deut. 18:10) soothsaying, (Deut. 18:10–26) enchanting, (Deut. 18:10–11) sorcery, (Deut. 18:10–11) charming, (Deut. 18:10–11) consulting ghosts or (Deut. 18:10–11) familiar spirits, and (Deut. 18:10–11) necromancy are forbidden. Women must not (Deut. 22:5) wear male clothing nor men [clothing] (Deut. 22:5) of women. Do not (Lev. 19:28) tattoo yourself in the manner of the idolaters.

You may not wear (Deut. 22:11) garments made of both wool and linen, nor may you shave [with a razor] the sides of (Lev.

19:27) your head or (Lev. 19:27) your beard. Do not (Deut. 16:1, 14:1; Lev. 19:28) lacerate yourself over your dead.

It is forbidden to return to Egypt to (Deut. 17:16) dwell there permanently or to (Num. 15:39) indulge in impure thoughts or sights. You may not (Exod. 23:32; Deut. 7:2) make a pact with the seven Canaanite nations or (Deut. 20:16) save the life of any member of them. Do not (Deut. 7:2) show mercy to idolaters, (Exod. 23:33) permit them to dwell in the land of Israel, or (Deut. 7:3) intermarry with them. A Jewish woman may not (Deut. 23:4) marry an Ammonite or Moabite even if he converts to Judaism, and is to refuse [for reasons of genealogy alone] (Deut. 23:8) a descendant of Esau or (Deut. 23:8) an Egyptian who is a proselyte. It is prohibited to make (Deut. 23:7) peace with the Ammonite or Moabite nation.

The (Deut. 20:19) destruction of fruit trees even in times of war is forbidden, as is wanton waste at any time. Do not (Deut. 7:21) fear the enemy and do not (Deut. 25:19) forget the evil done by Amalek.

You must not (Lev. 24:16; Exod. 22:27) blaspheme the Holy Name, (Lev. 19:12) break an oath made by it, (Exod. 20:7) take it in vain, or (Lev. 22:32) profane it. Do not (Deut. 6:16) test Adonai, [who is] God.

You may not (Deut. 12:4) erase God's name from the holy texts or destroy institutions devoted to Divine worship. Do not (Deut. 21:23) allow the body of one hanged to remain so overnight.

Be not (Num. 18:5) lax in guarding the Temple.

The high priest must not enter the Temple (Lev. 16:2) indiscriminately; a priest with a physical blemish may not (Lev. 21:23) enter there at all or (Lev. 21:17) serve in the sanctuary, and even if the blemish is of a temporary nature, he may not (Lev. 21:18) participate in the service there until it has passed.

The Levites and the priests must not (Num. 18:3) interchange in their functions. Intoxicated persons may not (Lev. 10:9–11) enter the sanctuary or teach the Torah. It is forbidden for (Num. 18:4) non-priests, (Lev. 22:2) unclean priests, or (Lev. 21:6) priests who have performed the necessary ablution but are still within the time limit of their uncleanness to serve in the Temple. No unclean person may enter (Num. 5:3) the Temple or (Deut. 23:11) the Temple Mount.

The altar must not be made of (Exod. 20:25) hewn stones, nor may the ascent to it be by (Exod. 20:26) steps. The fire on it may not be (Lev. 6:6) extinguished, nor may any other but the specified incense be (Exod. 30:9) burned on the golden altar. You may not (Exod. 30:32) manufacture oil with the same ingredients and in the same proportions as the anointing oil, which itself (Exod. 30:32) may not be misused. Neither may you (Exod. 30:37) compound incense with the same ingredients and in the same proportions as that burnt on the altar. You must not (Exod. 25:15) remove the staves from the Ark, (Exod. 28:28) remove the breastplate from the ephod, or (Exod. 28:32) make any incision in the upper garment of the high priest.

It is forbidden to (Deut. 12:13) offer sacrifices or (Lev. 17:3–4) slaughter consecrated animals outside the Temple. You may not (Lev. 22:20) sanctify, (Lev. 22:22) slaughter, (Lev. 22:24) sprinkle the blood of, or (Lev. 22:22) burn the inner parts of a blemished animal even if the blemish is (Deut. 17:1) of a temporary nature and even if it is (Lev. 22:25) offered by Gentiles. It is forbidden to (Lev. 22:21) inflict a blemish on an animal consecrated for sacrifice.

Leaven or honey may not (Lev. 2:11) be offered on the altar, neither may (Lev. 2:13) anything unsalted. An animal received as the hire of a harlot or as the price of a dog (Deut. 23:19) may not be offered.

Do not (Lev. 22:28) kill an animal and its young on the same day.

It is forbidden to use (Lev. 5:11) olive oil or (Lev. 5:11) frankincense in the sin-offering or (Num. 5:15), in the jealousy-offering (*sotah*). You may not (Lev. 27:10) substitute sacrifices even (Lev. 27:26) from one category to the other. You may not (Num. 18:17) redeem the firstborn of permitted animals. It is forbidden to (Lev. 27:33) sell the tithe of the herd or (Lev. 27:28) sell or (Lev. 27:28) redeem a field consecrated by the *cherem* vow. When you slaughter a bird for a sin-offering you may not (Lev. 5:8) split its head.

It is forbidden to (Deut. 15:19) work with or (Deut. 15:19) shear a consecrated animal. You must not slaughter the paschal lamb (Exod. 34:25) while there is still leaven about; nor may you leave overnight (Exod. 23:10) those parts that are to be offered up or (Exod. 12:10) to be eaten. You may not leave any part of the festive offering (Deut. 16:4) until the third day or any part of the (Num. 9:13) second paschal lamb or (Lev. 22:30) the thanksgiving-offering until the morning.

It is forbidden to break a bone of (Exod. 12:46) the first or (Num. 9:12) second paschal lamb or (Exod. 12:46) to carry their flesh out of the house where it is being eaten. You must not (Lev. 6:10) allow the remains of the meal-offering to become leaven. It is also forbidden to eat the paschal (Exod. 12:9) raw or sodden or to allow (Exod. 12:45) an alien resident, (Exod. 12:48) an uncircumcised person, or an (Exod. 12:43) apostate to eat of it.

A ritually unclean person (Lev. 12:4) must not eat of holy things, nor may (Lev. 7:19) holy things that have become unclean be eaten. Sacrificial meat (Lev. 19:6–8) that is left after the time-limit or (Lev. 7:18) that was slaughtered with wrong intentions must not be eaten. The heave-offering must not be eaten by (Lev. 22:10) a nonpriest, (Lev. 22:10) a priest's sojourner or hired worker, (Lev. 22:10) an uncircumcised person, or (Lev. 22:4) an unclean priest. The daughter of a priest who is married to a nonpriest may not (Lev. 22:12) eat of holy things.

The meal-offering of the priest (Lev. 6:16) must not be eaten, neither may (Lev. 6:23) the flesh of the sin-offerings sacrificed within the sanctuary or (Deut. 14:3) consecrated animals that have become blemished. You may not eat the second tithe of (Deut. 12:17) corn, (Deut. 12:17) wine, or (Deut. 12:17) oil or (Deut. 12:17) unblemished firstlings outside Jerusalem. The priests may not eat the (Deut. 12:17) sin-offerings or the trespass-offerings outside the Temple courts or (Deut. 12:17) the flesh of the burnt-offering at all. The lighter sacrifices (Deut. 12:17) may not be eaten before the blood has been sprinkled. A nonpriest may not (Deut. 12:17) eat of the holiest sacrifices, and a priest (Exod. 29:33) may not eat the first fruits outside the Temple courts.

One may not eat (Deut. 26:14) the second tithe while in a state of impurity or (Deut. 26:14) in mourning; its redemption money (Deut. 26:14) may not be used for anything other than food and drink.

You must not (Lev. 22:15) eat untithed produce or (Exod. 22:28) change the order of separating the various tithes.

Do not (Deut. 23:22) delay payment of offerings—either freewill or obligatory—and do not (Exod. 23:15) come to the Temple on the pilgrim festivals without an offering.

Do not (Num. 30:3) break your word.

A priest may not marry (Lev. 21:7) a harlot, (Lev. 21:7) a woman who has been profaned from the priesthood, or (Lev. 21:7) a divorcee; the high priests must not (Lev. 21:14) marry a widow or (Lev. 21:15) take one as a concubine. Priests may not enter the sanctuary with (Lev. 10:6) overgrown hair of the head or (Lev. 10:6) with torn clothing; they must not (Lev. 10:7) leave the courtyard during the Temple service. An ordinary priest may not render himself (Lev. 21:1) ritually impure except for those relatives specified, and the high priest should not become impure (Lev. 21:11) for anyone in (Lev. 21:11) any way.

The tribe of Levi shall have no part in (Deut. 18:1) the division of the land of Israel or (Deut. 18:1) in the spoils of war.

It is forbidden (Deut. 14:1) to make onself bald as a sign of mourning for one's dead.

A Jew may not eat (Deut. 14:7) unclean cattle, (Lev. 11:11)

unclean fish, (Lev. 11:13) unclean fowl, (Deut. 14:19) creeping things that fly, (Lev. 11:41) creatures that creep on the ground, (Lev. 11:44) reptiles, (Lev. 11:42) worms found in fruit or produce, or (Lev. 11:43) any detestable creature.

An animal that dies naturally (Deut. 14:21) is forbidden for consumption, as is (Exod. 22:30) a torn or mauled animal. One must not eat (Deut. 12:23) any limb taken from a living animal. Also prohibited is (Gen. 32:33) the sinew of the thigh (*gid ha'nasheh*), as is (Lev. 7:26) blood and (Lev. 7:23) certain types of fat (*chelev*). It is forbidden (Exod. 23:19) to cook meat together with milk or (Exod. 34:26) to eat of such a mixture. It is also forbidden to eat (Exod. 21:28) of an ox condemned to stoning (even should it have been properly slaughtered).

One may not eat (Lev. 23:14) bread made of new corn or the new corn itself, either (Lev. 23:14) roasted or (Lev. 23:14) green, before the *omer* offering has been brought on the sixteenth of Nisan. You may not eat (Lev. 19:23) *orlah* or (Deut. 22:9) the growth of mixed planting in the vineyard. Any use of (Deut. 32:38) wine libations to idols is prohibted, as is (Lev. 19:26; Deut. 21:20) gluttony and drunkenness. One may not eat anything on (Lev. 23:29) the Day of Atonement. During Passover it is forbidden to eat (Exod. 13:3) leaven (*chametz*) or (Exod. 13:20) anything containing a mixture of such. This is also forbidden (Deut. 16:3) after the middle of the fourteenth of Nisan [the day before Passover]. During Passover no leaven may be (Exod. 13:7) seen or (Exod. 12:19) found in your possession.

A Nazirite may not drink (Num. 6:3) wine or any beverage made from grapes; he may not eat (Num. 6:3) grapes, (Num. 6:3) dried grapes, (Num. 6:4) grape seeds, or (Num. 6:4) grape peel. He may not render himself (Num. 6:7) ritually impure for his dead, nor may he (Lev. 21:11) enter a tent in which there is a corpse. He must not (Num. 6:5) shave his hair.

It is forbidden (Lev. 23:22) to reap the whole of a field without leaving the corners for the poor; it is also forbidden to (Lev. 19:9) gather up the ears of corn that fall during reaping or to harvest (Lev. 19:10) the misformed clusters of grapes, or (Lev. 19:10) the grapes that fall or to (Deut. 24:19) return to take a forgotten sheaf.

You must not (Lev. 19:19) sow different species of seed together or (Deut. 22:9) corn in a vineyard; it is also forbidden to (Lev. 19:19) crossbreed different species of animals or (Deut. 22:10) work with two different species yoked together.

You must not (Deut. 25:4) muzzle an animal working in a field to prevent it from eating.

It is forbidden to (Lev. 25:4) till the earth, (Lev. 25:4) to prune trees, (Lev. 25:5) to reap [in the usual manner] produce or (Lev. 25:5) fruit that has grown without cultivation in the seventh year (*shemittah*). One may also not (Lev. 25:11) till the earth or prune trees in the Jubilee year, when it is also forbidden to harvest [in the usual manner] (Lev. 25:11) produce or (Lev. 25:11) fruit that has grown without cultivation.

One may not (Lev. 25:23) sell one's landed inheritance in the land of Israel permanently or (Lev. 25:33) change the lands of the Levites or (Deut. 12:19) leave the Levites without support.

It is forbidden to (Deut. 15:2) demand repayment of a loan after the seventh year; you may not, however, (Deut. 15:9) refuse to lend to the poor because that year is approaching. Do not (Deut. 15:7) deny charity to the poor or (Deut. 15:13) send a Hebrew slave away empty-handed when he finishes his period of service. Do not (Exod. 22:24) dun your debtor when you know that he [or she] cannot pay. It is forbidden to (Lev. 25:37) lend to or (Deut. 23:20) borrow from another Jew at interest or (Exod. 22:24) to participate in an agreement involving intereset either as a guarantor, witness, or writer of the contract.

Do not (Lev. 19:13) delay in the payment of wages.

You may not (Deut. 24:10) take a pledge from a debtor by violence, (Deut. 24:12) keep a poor person's pledge when he [or she] needs it, (Deut. 24:17) take any pledge from a widow or (Deut. 24:10) from any debtor if he [or she] earns a living from it.

Kidnapping (Exod. 20:13) a Jew is forbidden.

Do not (Lev. 19:11) steal or (Lev. 19:13) rob by violence. Do not (Deut. 19:14) remove a land marker or (Lev. 19:13) defraud.

It is forbidden (Lev. 19:11) to deny receipt of a loan or a deposit or (Lev. 19:11) to swear falsely regarding another person's property.

You must not (Lev. 25:14) decieve anyone in business. You may not (Lev. 25:17) mislead a person even (Exod. 22:20) verbally or (Exod. 20:20) do him [or her] injury in trade.

You may not (Deut. 23:16) return or (Deut. 23:17) otherwise take advantage of a slave who has fled to the land of Israel from his master, even if his master is a Jew.

Do not (Exod. 22:21) afflict the widow or the orphan. You may not (Lev. 25:39) misuse or (Lev. 25:42) sell a Hebrew slave; do not (Lev. 25:43) treat him cruelly or (Lev. 25:53) allow a heathen to mistreat him. You must not (Exod. 21:8) sell your Hebrew maidservant or, if you marry her, (Exod. 21:10) withhold food, clothing, and conjugal rights from her. You must not (Deut. 21:14) sell a female captive or (Deut. 21:14) treat her as a slave.

Do not covet (Exod. 20:17) another person's possessions even if you are willing to pay for them. Even (Deut. 5:18) the desire alone is forbidden.

A worker must not (Deut. 23:26) cut down standing corn during his [or her] work or (Deut. 23:25) take more fruit than he [or she] can eat.

One must not (Deut. 22:3) turn away from a lost article, which is to be returned to its owner, nor may you (Exod. 23:5) refuse to help a person on an animal that is collapsing under its burden.

It is forbidden to (Lev. 19:35) defraud with weights and measures or even (Deut. 25:13) to possess inaccurate weights.

A judge must not (Lev. 19:15) perpetrate injustice, (Exod. 23:8) accept bribes, or be (Lev. 19:15) partial or (Deut. 1:17) afraid. He [or she] may (Lev. 19:15; Exod. 23:3) not favor the poor or (Exod. 23:6) discriminate against the wicked; he [or she] should not (Deut. 19:13) pity the condemned or (Deut. 24:17) pervert the judgment of strangers or orphans.

It is forbidden to (Exod. 23:1) hear one litigant without the other being present. A capital case cannot be decided by (Exod. 23:2) a majority of one.

A judge must not (Exod. 23:2) accept a colleague's opinion unless he [or she] is convinced of its correctness; it is forbidden to (Deut. 1:17) appoint as a judge someone who is ignorant of the law.

Do not (Exod. 20:16) give false testimony or accept (Exod. 23:1) testimony from a wicked person or from (Deut. 24:16) relatives of a person involved in the case. It is forbidden to pronounce judgment (Deut. 19:15) on the basis of the testimony of one witness.

Do not (Exod. 20:13) murder.

You must not convict on (Exod. 23:7) circumstantial evidence alone.

A witness (Num. 35:30) must not sit as a judge in capital cases. You must not (Num. 35:12) execute anyone without due proper trial and conviction.

Do not (Deut. 25:12) pity or spare the pursuer.

Punishment is not to be inflicted for (Deut. 22:26) an act committed under duress.

Do not accept ransom (Num. 35:31) for a murderer or (Num. 35:32) a manslayer.

Do not (Lev. 19:16) hesitate to save another person from danger, and do not (Deut. 22:8) leave a stumbling block in the way or (Lev. 19:14) mislead another person by giving wrong advice.

It is forbidden (Deut. 25:2–3) to administer more than the assigned number of lashes to the guilty.

Do not (Lev. 19:16) tell tales or (Lev. 19:17) bear hatred in your heart. It is forbidden to (Lev. 19:17) shame a Jew, (Lev. 19:18) to bear a grudge, or (Lev. 19:18) to take revenge.

Do not (Deut. 22:6) take the mother when you take the young birds.

It is forbidden to (Lev. 13:33) shave a leprous scale or (Deut. 24:8) remove other signs of that affliction. It is forbidden (Deut. 21:4) to cultivate a valley in which a slain body was found and in which subsequently the ritual of breaking the heifer's neck (*egla arufah*) was performed.

Do not (Exod. 22:17) suffer a witch to live.

Do not (Deut. 24:5) force a bridegroom to perform military service during the first year of his marriage. It is forbidden to (Deut. 17:11) rebel against the transmitters of the tradition or to (Deut. 13:1) add or (Deut. 13:1) detract from the precepts of the Torah.

Do not curse (Exod. 22:27) a judge, (Exod. 22:27) a ruler, or (Lev. 19:14) any Jew. Do not (Exod. 21:17) curse or (Exod. 21:15) strike a parent.

It is forbidden to (Exod. 20:10) work on the Sabbath or (Exod. 16:29) to walk farther than the permitted limits (*eruv*). You may not (Exod. 35:3) inflict punishment on the Sabbath.

It is forbidden to work on (Exod. 12:16) the first or (Exod. 12:16) the seventh day of Passover, on (Lev. 23:21) Shavuot, on (Lev. 23:25) Rosh Hashanah, on the (Lev. 23:35) first and (Lev. 23:36) eighth (*Shemini Atzeret*) days of Sukkot, and (Lev. 23:28) on the Day of Atonement.

It is forbidden to enter into an incestuous relationship with one's (Lev. 18:7) mother, (Lev. 18:8) stepmother, (Lev. 18:9) sister, (Lev. 18:11) half-sister, (Lev. 18:10) son's daughter, (Lev. 18:10) daughter's daughter, (Lev. 18:10) daughter, (Lev. 18:17) any woman and her daughter, (Lev. 18:17) any woman and her son's daughter, (Lev. 18:17) any woman and her daughter's daughter, (Lev. 18:12) father's sister, (Lev. 18:13) mother's sister, (Lev. 18:14) paternal uncle's wife, (Lev. 18:15) daughter-in-law, (Lev. 18:16) brother's wife, or (Lev. 18:18) wife's sister.

It is also forbidden to (Lev. 18:19) have sexual relations with a menstruous woman.

Do not (Lev. 18:20) commit adultery.

It is forbidden for (Lev. 18:23) a man or (Lev. 18:23) a woman to have sexual intercourse with an animal.

Homosexuality (Lev. 18:22) is forbidden, particularly with (Lev. 18:7) one's father or (Lev. 18:14) uncle.

It is forbidden to have (Lev. 18:6) intimate physical contact (even without actual intercourse) with any of the women with whom intercourse is forbidden.

A *mamzer* (illegitimate child) may not marry (Deut. 23:3) a Jewish woman.

Prostitution (Deut. 23:18) is forbidden.

A divorcee may not be (Deut. 24:4) remarried to her first husband if, in the meanwhile, she has married another.

A childless widow may not (Deut. 25:5) marry anyone other than her late husband's brother.

A man may not (Deut. 22:29) divorce a wife whom he married after having raped her or (Deut. 22:19) after having slandered her.

A eunuch may not (Deut. 23:2) marry a Jewish woman.

Castration (Lev. 22:24) is forbidden.

You may not (Deut. 17:15) elect as king anyone who is not of the seed of Israel.

The king may not accumulate an excessive number of (Deut. 17:16) horses, (Deut. 17:17) wives, or (Deut. 17:17) wealth.

DETAILS

According to the Talmud (*Makkot* 23b), there are 613 commandments. Rabbi Simlai stated: "Six hundred and thirteen commandments were given to Moses; three hundred and sixty-five negative commandments, corresponding to the numbers of days in the solar year, and two hundred and forty-eight positive commandments, corresponding to the number of parts of the human body."

This tradition was generally accepted as the legal framework for the codification of Jewish law.

THE SIX HUNDRED THIRTEEN COMMANDMENTS IN A NUTSHELL

The actual enumeration of the 613 commandments first appear in the Jewish legal compendium entitled *Halakhot Gedolot*, produced during the gaonic period. This work also classifies the commandments according to the degree of punishment incurred by transgressing them and according to their common character.

Among the foremost of the codes of law that groups the commandments using the 613 mitzvot system is the *Sefer HaHinnuch*, the *Book of Education*, which is attributed to the thirteenth-century scholar Rabbi Aaron HaLevi of Barcelona. This book deals with the legal aspects of the commandments and also attempts to understand their religious and ethical roots. In his introduction to the *Sefer HaHinnuch*, the author states that the precepts applicable in our time to all Jews on various occasions total 270: affirmative, 48; negative, 222. The six precepts that are of continuous application concern the belief in the only One God, who is to be loved and revered always.

In the nineteenth century, Rabbi Israel Meir haCohen, known as the Hafetz Hayim, wrote a book called *Sefer HaMitzvot Hakatzar* (*The Short Book of the Commandments*). In it he includes a listing of both the positive and the negative commandments that are still applicable today.

67

SODOM AND GOMORRAH

And God said: Verily the cry of Sodom and Gomorrah is great, and their sin is grievous. I will go down and see whether they have done altogether according to the cry of it, which is come unto Me.

—Genesis 20:21

DETAILS

The destruction of the cities of Sodom and Gomorrah is referred to so frequently in the Bible that only a historic cataclysm of immense proportions could have impressed itself so deeply on popular memory. The two cities most likely stood on the south end of the present Dead Sea (where today's Sodom is situated). The district is filled with bitumen and salt formations and is part of a deep rift that reaches from Armenia to Central Africa and that runs north-south through the Aravah Valley.

In the story, God destroys the people of Sodom and Gomorrah because they were evil. The rabbis conjectured that their evil was related to sexual depravity.

SODOM AND GOMORRAH IN A NUTSHELL

The story of Sodom and Gomorrah presents us with the first human being to ever argue with God. Abraham pleads with God on behalf of the righteous in Sodom and Gomorrah. He starts bargaining with God, asking that God spare the cities if righteous people can be found. When it becomes apparent that the entire population of the cities is evil, God proceeds to destroy them. The story of Sodom and Gomorrah thus introduces the concept of merit, stipulating that a handful of concerned and righteous people could have averted Sodom's destruction by their merit.

In his pursuit of divine equity, Abraham does not go below the number ten. The Rabbis advised that if one could not find ten religiously minded people in a city one should move away. They also set ten as the minimal number required for communal worship (i.e., a *minyan*).

68

SONG OF THE SEA

Then Moses and the people of Israel sang this song to God:

I will sing to the Lord, mighty in majestic triumph

Horse and driver God has cast into the sea.

God is my strength and my might; God is my deliverance.

He is my God and I will glorify Him,

My father's God and I will exalt Him.

The Lord, the Warrior, His name is the Lord.

Pharaoh's chariots and army God has cast into the sea.

Pharaoh's choice captains and sunk in the Sea of Reeds.

The depths cover them. They sink in the deep like stone.

Your right hand, God, singular in strength,

Your right hand, God, shatters the foe.

With your majestic might You crush Your enemies.

You let loose Your fury, to consume them like straw.

In the rush of Your rage the waters were raised;

The sea stood still, the great deep congealed.

The enemy said: "I will pursue and plunder,

I will devour them, I will draw my sword,

With my bare hands will I dispatch them."

You loosed the wind, the sea covered them;

They sank like lead in the swelling waters.

Who is like You, God, among all that is worshiped?

Who is like You, majestic in holiness,

Awesome in splendor, working wonders?

You stretched out Your hand, the earth swallowed them.

In Your love You lead the people You redeemed,

With your strength You guide them to Your holy abode.

Nations pay attention and tremble,

Panic grips the people of Philistia.

Edom's chieftains are chilled with dismay,

Trembling seizes the mighty of Moab,

All the citizens of Canaan are confused,

Dread and dismay descend upon them.

Your overwhelming power makes them still as stone,

While Your people, God, pass peacefully through,

The people whom You have redeemed.

You bring them in and plant them,

In the mountain of Your inheritance.

The place, O God, which You have made for You to dwell in

The sanctuary, O God, which Your hands have established.

The Lord shall reign forever and forever.

—Exodus 15:1–18

DETAILS

The spectacular fleeing of the Israelites from the pursuing Egyptians forms the conclusion of the tale of liberation. After four hundred years of Egyptian slavery, the Egyptian Pharaoh released the Israelites after God's plague of slaying the firstborn sons appeared to break his will. After the Israelites hastily made their exit, Pharaoh's chariots were in hot pursuit. Soon it became obvious that the Sea of Reeds stood in the way of freedom for the Israelites. It was then that God said to Moses: "Lift up your rod and stretch out your hand over the sea and divide it. And the children of Israel shall go into the midst of the sea on dry ground (Exodus 14:16).

Moses followed God's command, the sea parted, and the Israelites escaped to safety while the Egyptians drowned.

A magnificent hymn of praise (Exodus 15:1–18) was chanted by Moses and the people of Israel at the Red Sea.

SONG OF THE SEA IN A NUTSHELL

The Song of the Sea consists of three stanzas of increasing length, giving expression to the mingled feelings of horror, triumph, and gratitude of Israelite slaves pursued by Egyptian hordes and delivered by their redeeming God. This song of the sea, known in Hebrew as *shirat ha-yam*, forms part of the daily morning service, at the end of the biblical poetic passages known as *pesukai dezimrah,* in keeping with the precept to "remember the day you left Egypt all the days of your life" (Deuteronomy 16:3). Mystic tradition states that one who recites the Song of the Sea audibly and joyously is pardoned in heaven (Sefer Haredim). It is one of the finest codes in the Bible as to glowing diction and vivid imagery.

69
THE *TALLIT*—PRAYER SHAWL

Instruct the people of Israel that in every generation they shall put fringes on the corners of their garments and bind a thread of blue to the fringe of each corner. Looking upon it, you will always be reminded of all the mitzvot of God and fulfill them and not be led astray by your eyes. Then you will remember and observe all My mitzvot and be holy before your God. I am Adonai your God, who brought you out of the land of Egypt to be your God. I, Adonai, am your God.

—Numbers 15:37–41

DETAILS

The *tallit* is a four-cornered garment, usually made of wool, upon the corners of which fringes *(tzitzit)* have been knotted in accordance with the biblical prescription (Numbers 15:37–41). The term *tallit* itself is derived from the Hebrew-Aramaic verb *tallal* ("to cover"). In the Talmud it is frequently used in the sense of a cloak, a loose outer garment worn by men. But the special and most popular significance of *tallit* is assigned to the cloak of honor, adorned with fringes (*tzitzit* in Hebrew), in keeping with the

187

biblical command to put fringes on the corners of the garments, the sight of which is to remind the Jew to observe all of the religious obligations.

Rectangular in form, the prayer shawl is worn today by men (and some women too), usually during morning prayer. (The exception to this is the Kol Nidrei service on the eve of the Day of Atonement.) Traditionally, only boys who reach the age of Bar Mitzvah or married men in traditional settings wear a *tallit*. Many traditional boys wear a *tallit katan* (a small *tallit*) under their shirts all day and a large *tallit* just for morning prayers. The small *tallit* is placed over the head like a poncho. Since the biblical verse instructs that the fringes be seen, some traditional Jews make sure that the fringes of their small *tallit* hang out.

The blue cord entwined in the fringe mentioned in the Book of Numbers was originally its chief distinction. According to the talmudic tractate of *Menachot* 43b, the color blue was chosen because it resembled the sea, and the sea resembles the sky. When, however, it became impossible to procure the special dye required, it was made permissible to use white threads alone. (Recently an aquatic mollusk was discovered, which some rabbinic authorities say secretes a dye similar to the color used back in biblical times. Today it is possible to purchase fringes with this blue color.)

THE *TALLIT*—PRAYER SHAWL—IN A NUTSHELL

Before putting on the *tallit*, some people say the following verses from the Book of Psalms to heighten their desire to put on a *tallit*: "Bless my soul, Adonai. You are very great, clothed in glory and majesty. You are very great, clothed in glory and majesty, wrapped in a robe of light. You spread the heavens like a tent cloth (Psalm 104:1–20). Next, the *tallit* is spread open with the *atara* (neckband) facing the person. This blessing is then said:

Baruch atah Adonai elohaynu melech ha'olam asher kidshanu bemitzvotav vetzivanu l'hitatef ba'tzitzit.

Praised are You, Adonai our God, Sovereign of the Universe, who has made us holy with mitzvot and instructed us to wrap ourselves with *tzitzit.*

Some people have the custom of kissing each end of the neckpiece after the blessing. Others may wrap the head briefly with the *tallit* for a moment of meditation.

Finally, many people follow the custom of bringing the *tzitzit* to their lips and kissing them each of the three times that the word *tzitzit* is mentioned when reading the third paragraph of the Shema (Numbers 15:37–41).

TALLIT SYMBOLISM IN A NUTSHELL

In *gematria* (Jewish numerology), the Hebrew word *tzitzit* has the number value of 600. In addition, there are eight strands plus five double knots for each *tzitzit*. This totals 613, which is the exact number of commandments in the Torah. Thus the *tzitzit* are in a sense a kind of string around one's finger providing a constant reminder to Jews of God's commandments.

The wound spirals in each *tzitzit* are seven, eight, eleven, and thirteen. Seven plus eight equals fifteen, which in *gematria* is equal to the letters *yod* and *hey*, the first two letters of God's name. Eleven is the equivalent of the Hebrew letters *vav* and *hey*—the last two letters of God's name. The combined total of twenty-six is representative of the four-letter name of God, YHVH. Thirteen is the number value of the Hebrew word *echad*, which means "One." Thus, to look at the *tzitzit* is to always be reminded that God is One, YHVH *echad.*

70

TALMUD TORAH—STUDY OF TORAH

You shall love the Lord your God with all your heart, and all your soul and all your might. Take to heart these instructions with which I charge you this day. Impress them upon your children. Recite them when you stay at home and when you are away, when you lie down and when you rise up.

—Deuteronomy 6:5–7

DETAILS

Because the Torah is the touchstone of the Jewish people, Jews are often called "the people of the book." The book of course is the Torah, the Five Books of Moses. But Torah is more than just one book. It can also refer to all of Jewish sacred literature and learning. The rabbis emphasized the study of Torah because they believed that Torah study leads a person to the observance of other mitzvot.

In the first paragraph of the Shema, which is derived from the Book of Deuteronomy 6:4–8, the Jew is charged to express his or her love for God through constant study: "When you lie down and when you rise up." Such study has the potential to bring the people into a closer relationship with God. Torah study sweetens one's life. To emphasize this sweetness, children, especially in Eastern Europe, used to begin their study of Hebrew with letters that had been written in honey. As they learned the letters and enjoyed the honey, they also learned that the study of Torah was sweet.

TORAH—STUDY OF TORAH— IN A NUTSHELL

We find the instruction to study Torah wherever we turn in Jewish tradition. Torah study was encouraged not only to sharpen one's mind, but also to serve as a guide for living a moral life. The logic goes this way: One who takes Torah study seriously will most likely choose the right path in life. For this reason, the mitzvah of Torah study outweighs all other commandments. The rabbis of the Talmud wrote: "These are the things for which a person enjoys the dividends in this world while the principal remains for the person to enjoy in the world-to-come. They are: honoring parents, loving deeds of kindness, making peace between one person and another, but the study of the Torah is equal to them all" (Talmud *Shabbat* 127a).

Here are some statements from rabbinic tradition that aptly sum up the importance of Torah study.

- "The world stands on three things: on Torah, worship and loving deeds of kindness (Ethics of the Fathers 1:2).
- "Make your home a regular meeting place for scholars" (Ethics of the Fathers 1:4).
- "Be a disciple of Aaron: love peace and pursue it; love your neighbors and attract them to Torah" (Ethics of the Fathers 1:12).
- "Shammai taught: Make the study of Torah your primary pursuit" (Ethics of the Fathers 1:15).

- "One who has acquired Torah has acquired eternal life" (Ethics of the Fathers 2:8).
- "If you have studied much Torah, your reward will be abundant" (Ethics of the Fathers 2:21).
- "The Torah is a tree of life to those who cling to it. All who uphold it are happy" (Proverbs 3:18).
- "If you truly wish your children to study Torah, study it yourself in their presence. They will follow your example. Otherwise, they will not themselves study Torah but will simply instruct their children to do so" (Rabbi Menahem Mendel of Kotzk).

71
TEFILLIN—PHYLACTERIES

And it shall serve you as a sign on your hand and as a reminder on your forehead—in order that the teachings of Adonai may be in your mouth—that with a mighty hand Adonai freed you from Egypt.

—Exodus 13:9

And so it shall be as a sign upon your hand and as a symbol on your forehead that with a mighty hand Adonai freed us from Egypt.

—Exodus 13:16

Bind them as a sign on your hand and let them serve as a symbol on your forehead.

—Exodus 13:16

Therefore impress these My words upon your very heart. Bind them as a sign on your hand and let them serve as a symbol on your forehead.

—Deuteronomy 11:18

193

DETAILS

The term *tefillin* is reminiscent of the word *tefillah*, Hebrew for prayer. Tefillin (or phylacteries) are two small black boxes with black straps attached to them. According to rabbinic law, Jewish men are required to place one box (called the "shel rosh") on one's head and tie the other (called the "shel yad") on their arm each weekday morning. The text on the parchment that is inserted in each of the two boxes are passages from Exodus 13:1–10 and 11–16, Deuteronomy 6:4–9, and Deuteronomy 11:13–20. These texts stress the duty of loving and serving God with one's whole being and demand that one give living expression to one's love of God by careful observance of God's precepts, which are designed to assure happiness.

The tefillin are worn by Jewish males from the age of thirteen during the daily morning service. (Some women also choose to wear tefillin as well.) Tefillin are not worn on Sabbaths and festivals, which themselves bear witness to the sacred ideas that are enshrined in the tefillin and are referred to as signs between God and his people. At one time the saintly scholars wore tefillin the whole day.

TEFILLIN—PHYLACTERIES— IN A NUTSHELL

Tefillin are leather boxes attached to straps. When placed on the head between one's eyes and wrapped around one's arm, they symbolically bind both one's mind and body to God. Tefillin are only worn during the Shacharit (morning) service. Traditionally, only boys who reach the age of Bar Mitzvah wear tefillin. Some girls who reach the age of Bat Mitzvah also choose to wear tefillin.

Tefillin are not worn on the Sabbath or major festivals, since holidays themselves are a sign of a person's relationship with God.

Tefillin have become a sign of one's connection with God on ordinary days.

The *tallit* (prayer shawl) is always put on before tefillin, because it is worn every day of the year while tefillin are worn only on ordinary days. Some people follow the custom of touching the tefillin box with their fingers and bringing their fingers to their lips as a kiss when they say "bind them for a sign" during the Shema Yisrael prayer in the morning.

72

TELLING THE STORY OF THE EXODUS

And you shall tell your son on that day saying: "It is because of that which the Lord did for me when I came forth out of Egypt."

—Exodus 13:8

DETAILS

This biblical commandment refers to the important event of the Passover seder, when, using the book called the Haggadah, families retell the story of the Israelites' exodus from Egypt. The story of Passover must be told on the level of a child, so that even a very young one is able to comprehend it. According to Jewish law, if a man has neither children nor a wife, he must still celebrate the seder and ask and answer the questions himself.

TELLING THE STORY OF THE EXODUS IN A NUTSHELL

Nearly all the fundamental precepts of Judaism are linked to the historic event of Israel's exodus from Egypt. The most enduring meaning of the exodus is suggested by the Ten Com-

196

mandments, which begin with the words: "I am the Lord your God who brought you out of the land of Egypt."

It is a religious obligation for a parent to tell the story of the exodus from Egypt to one's child or children. The story clearly demonstrates the dependability of a God who can truly perform wonders. The entire story of the exodus from Egypt is found in the Passover Haggadah, the recital of which is the most indispensable part of the seder service on the night of Passover. The Haggadah tells the story of the entry into Egypt and the liberation of the Israelites from their servitude there. It explains the use of the paschal lamb during Temple times, the matzah (unleavened bread), and the *maror* (bitter herbs).

73
TEN COMMANDMENTS

1. I am the Lord your God who brought you out of the land of Egypt, the house of bondage.

2. You shall have no other gods besides Me.

3. You shall not carry the Lord your God's name in vain.

4. Remember the Sabbath day to make it holy.

5. Honor your mother and your father.

6. You shall not murder.

7. You shall not commit adultery.

8. You shall not steal.

9. You shall not bear false witness against your neighbor.

10. You shall not covet your neighbor's house. You shall not covet your neighbor's wife, or . . . anything that is your neighbor's.

—Exodus 20:2–14

[Note: a somewhat differently worded version of the Ten Commandments is found in Deuteronomy 5:6–18.]

DETAILS

The Ten Commandments represent a summary of universal duties that are binding upon the entire human species. They cover the whole religious and moral life, affirming the existence of God and prohibiting idolatry and the profane use of the divine name. They stress the importance of the Sabbath and the reverence due to one's parents. They forbid murder, adultery, theft, false testimony, and predatory desires.

Primarily contained in Exodus 20:2–27, the Ten Commandments reappear in a somewhat modified form in Deuteronomy 5:6–21, where the Sabbath is based upon the deliverance from Egypt, instead of God resting on the seventh day from the work of creation, and the word *desire* is used in place of *covet*. It has been suggested by some Bible scholars that, like the last five commandments, each of the first five was originally brief, containing merely the precept without the reason annexed. The elaboration and the minor variations came later.

TEN COMMANDMENTS IN A NUTSHELL

Sociologically, if not religiously, the Ten Commandments are the most significant element in the Bible. These few brief commands, only 120 words in all, cover the entire gamut of human conduct, not only of outer actions but also of the inner thoughts of the heart. According to a talmudic statement (*Berachot* 12a), the Ten Commandments were recited in the Jerusalem Temple as part of the daily liturgy, before the prayer Shema.

A dual structure can be seen in the Ten Commandments. Commandments one through four deal with man's relationship to God, while commandments six through ten deal with man's relation to man. The fifth command, that of honoring one's parents, forms a sort of bridge between the two groups.

Some commentators viewed the Ten Commandments as ranging in descending order from divine matters to human matters and within each group from higher to lower values. In this scenario, duties to God come first, the obligation to worship God alone precedes that of treating God's name with reverence, and both precede the symbolic piety of Sabbath rest. Respect for parental authority naturally follows respect for God. The purely ethical commandments are arranged in a hierarchal form: life, the family, right of possession, reliability of public statements. The last commandment, the ban on desires arising from jealousy, deals with what is most ethically sensitive and protects against the infringing of the other ethical commandments.

Today the Ten Commandments are included as additional readings in Reform, Conservative, Orthodox, and Reconstructionist prayerbooks. Perhaps this ambivalent status of including them in this way arose from the fear that it might be considered that the Ten Commandments were the sole essence of Judaism and that other commandments could be discarded. The Ten Commandments are also read as part of the regular weekly Torah portions (twice a year in the portions Yitro [Exodus 19–20] and Va'etchanan (Deuteronomy 5] and on the festival of Shavuot. The custom is for the congregation to rise when the Ten Commandments are being read.

74
THE TEN PLAGUES

DETAILS

As a result of the Israelite afflictions suffered by the Egyptians because of Pharaoh's refusal to permit the Israelites to leave the country, God sent ten plagues upon the Egyptians. They were: 1. the waters of the Nile turned to blood; 2. infestation of frogs; 3. lice affecting man and beast; 4. flies; 5. murrain affecting the cattle; 6. boils; 7. heavy hail; 8. locusts devouring the crops; 9. three days of darkness; 10. death of the firstborn of man and beast.

Seven plagues were brought on by Moses or Aaron raising his staff and three were sent directly by God.

THE TEN PLAGUES IN A NUTSHELL

The Bible story is extremely vivid and graphic in its portrayal of the Ten Plagues. Pharaoh's strength collides with the inexhaustible resources of nature, which Moses is permitted to wield.

Instead of annihilating the Egyptians by one mighty stroke, God, in His divine forbearance, inflicts ten successive plagues to break Pharaoh's pride. Ten times Pharaoh is warned by God, and ten times God gave him respite to repent. Pharaoh's stubbornness leads to the ultimate humiliation of his army as they drown in the Sea of Reeds, the Israelites having crossed safely by virtue of God's miraculous splitting of the Sea.

The recitation of the Ten Plagues, found in the Passover Haggadah and recited aloud during the seder, are a reminder of perhaps the greatest miracle in biblical times—the escape of the Israelites from 400 years of Egyptian bondage.

75

Test of the Staffs

And the Lord spoke to Moses saying: "Speak to the children of Israel, and take the rods, one for each father's house, of all their princes according to their fathers' houses, twelve rods. Write every person's name upon his rod. And you shall write Aaron's name upon the rod of Levi, for there shall be one rod for the head of their fathers' houses. And you shall lay them up in the tent of meeting before the testimony, where I meet with you. And it shall come to pass, that the man whom I shall choose, his rod shall bud. And I will make to cease from Me the murmurings of the children of Israel, which they murmur against you." And Moses spoke to the children of Israel. And all their princes gave him rods, for each prince one, according to their fathers' houses, even twelve rods. And the rod of Aaron was among their rod. And Moses laid up the rods before the Lord in the tent of the testimony. And it came to pass on the morrow, that Moses went into the tent of the testimony. And behold, the rod of Aaron for the house of Levi was budded, and put forth buds, and bloomed blossoms, and bore ripe almonds.

And Moses brought out all the rods from before the Lord unto all the children of Israel. And they looked, and took every man his rod. And the Lord said unto Moses: "Put back the rod of Aaron before the testimony, to be kept there, for a token against the rebellious children. That there may be made an end of their murmurings against Me, and they die not." Thus did Moses as God commanded him, so did he.

—Numbers 17:1–11

DETAILS

After Korach and his followers tried to wrest the leadership from Moses, they were killed by an earthquake. However, more persuasion was necessary if all the Israelites were to be thoroughly convinced that Aaron had been chosen above "God's people" (Numbers 17:6). The test of the staff was created to settle this issue of doubt once and for all. The staff of Aaron sprouted and produced blossoms.

TEST OF THE STAFFS IN A NUTSHELL

Throughout history, staffs have been used as symbols of authority (the scepter of a monarch, the baton of an orchestra conductor, and so forth). Aaron's staff, which had been turned into a snake and had been the signal for turning the Nile River into blood, was probably a fairly ordinary stick. In the story of the test of the rods in the Book of Numbers, the Bible clearly interprets the overnight budding of Aaron's rod as nothing short of a miracle. Late legends (such as the stick of Joseph and Arimathea and that of Hercules) continue to use the theme of the sprouting stick.

The Midrash (Numbers Rabbah 18:23) says that the same staff of Aaron will be destined to be held in the hand of the King Messiah.

76
TITHES

You shall set aside every year a tenth part of all the yield of your sowing that is brought from the field. You shall consume the tithes of your new grain and wine and oil, and the firstlings of your herds and flocks, in the presence of the Lord your God, in the place where God will choose to establish His name, so that you may learn to revere the Lord your God forever. Should the distance be too great for you, should you be unable to transport them, because the place where the Lord your God has chosen to establish His name is far from you and because the Lord your God has blessed you, you may convert them into money. Wrap up the money and take it with you to the place that the Lord your God has chosen . . . Every third year you shall bring out the full tithe of your yield of that year, but leave it within your settlements.

—Deuteronomy 14:22–27

DETAILS

According to this biblical passage, tithing is to be an annual process, and its portions were eaten at the sanctuary. If the distance from one's home was too great, the produce could be converted into money, and with the proceeds the food for the feast could be purchased at the locale of the sanctuary. Every third year, however, the tithe was kept in the home community and distributed to the Levites and the poor, who depended on such contributions for their very survival.

TITHES IN A NUTSHELL

The concept of tithing and giving a portion of one's bounty as an expression of gratitude to God is an ancient one. In the Book of Genesis, Jacob vows to tithe if God will offer him protection (Genesis 28:22).

During the time of the Second Temple, tithes were no longer given to the Levites and instead were presented directly to the priests. The laws concerning tithing are contained in a number of mishnaic and Palestinian talmudic treatises, notably Terumot, Demai, Ma'aserot, and Ma'aser Sheni.

77
TOWER OF BABEL

Everyone on earth had the same language and the same words. As they migrated from the east, they came upon a valley in the land of Shinar and settled there. They said to one another, "Come, let us make bricks and burn them hard." Brick served them as stone, and bitumen served them as mortar. And they said, "Come, let us build us a city, and a tower with its top in the sky, to make a name for ourselves; else we be scattered all over the world." God came down to look at the city and tower that man had built. And God said, "If, as one people with one language for all, this is how they have begun to act, then nothing that they may propose to do will be out of their reach. Let us, then, go down and confound their speech, so that they shall not understand one another's speech." Thus the Lord scattered them from there over the face of the whole earth, and they stopped building the city. That is why it was called Babel, because God confounded the speech of the whole earth. And from there God scattered them over the face of the whole earth.

—Genesis 11:1–9

208

DETAILS

A tower-like structure called *zikurat*, literally "that which has been raised high," was a distinctive feature of all Babylonian temple complexes and may have served as the human constructed equivalent of the mythical holy mountain in Babylonian mythology. This tower-like structure was reported to have consisted of seven stories, reaching a height of nearly three hundred feet. Archaeologists have uncovered the foundation of this tower, and its extent appears to coincide with the reputed size of the Tower of Babel.

The Bible's contempt for the paganism of Babylon determined the interpretation of the catastrophe that befell the city and its tower. Babel, as the Hebrew word *bavel* suggests, truly turned out to be a place of confusion.

TOWER OF BABEL IN A NUTSHELL

It has been observed that the biblical story cannot mean that the erection of the tower had as its only purpose the diversity of languages. It shows rather the futility of human attempts to maintain unity by material means alone, excluding God. From the earliest times the splendid buildings of Babylonia were among the most remarkable achievements of human power and pride. Hence Babylon was seen as the emblem of grandiose ambition and despotic arrogance. Confounding the human language was an assurance that the Babel incident would never be repeated.

78

Twelve Tribes of Israel

According to the Bible (Genesis 49), the patriarch Jacob's twelve sons eventually became the twelve tribes of Israel. They were: Reuben, Simeon, Levi, Judah, Issachar, Zebulun, Joseph, Benjamin, Dan, Naphtali, Gad, and Asher. Since Moses conferred the priestly office on the tribe of Levi (without land), he transferred the property rights of Joseph to his children, Ephraim and Manasseh, to maintain the number of tribes receiving territory at twelve (a sacred number).

DETAILS

Just as all mankind descend from Adam and Eve, Jews all descend from the patriarchs. The twelve tribes of Israel were derived from the twelve sons of Jacob. Following is a summary of the blessing that Jacob gave to each of his sons as he was lying on his death bed:

Jacob called his sons and said: "Gather together that I may tell you what will happen to you in the end of days. Reuben, you are my first-born. My might and the first fruits of my strength. Unstable as water, you shall excel no longer, for when you mounted your father's bed you brought disgrace.

Simeon and Levi are a pair. Their weapons are tools of lawlessness. Cursed be their anger so fierce, and their wrath so relentless. I will divide them in Jacob and scatter them in Israel.

You, O Judah, your brothers shall praise. Judah is a lion's whelp. The scepter shall not depart from Judah, nor the ruler's staff from between his feet.

Zebulun shall dwell by the shore of the sea, and he shall be a shore of ships and his flank shall be upon Zidon.

Issachar is a strong-boned ass, crouching among the sheepfolds.

Dan shall govern his people as one of the tribes of Israel. He shall be a serpent by the road, a viper by the path that bites the horse's heels so that his rider is thrown backward.

Gad shall be raided by raiders, but he shall raid at their heels.

Asher's bread shall be rich, and he shall yield royal dainties.

Naphtali is a hind let loose which yields beautiful fawns.

Joseph is a wild ass. Archers bitterly assailed him yet his bow stayed taut and his arms were made firm by the hands of the Mighty One of Jacob.

Benjamin is a ravenous wolf. In the morning he consumes the foe and in the evening he divides the spoil." All these were the tribes of Israel, twelve in number, and this is what their father said to them as he bade them farewell. (Genesis 49:1-28)

Moses conferred the priestly office on the tribe of Levi, and to maintain the number of tribes receiving territory at twelve (a sacred number), divided the tribe of Joseph into the tribes of Ephraim and Manasseh. Under Joshua, Reuben, Gad, and half of the tribe of

Manasseh received territory in Transjordan; Naphtali and Asher on the Sidonian frontier in Galilee; Issachar and Zebulun in the Valley of Jezreel area; Ephraim and the other half of Manasseh in the mountains of Samaria, with Benjamin to their south, and Judah further south. Dan was along the seacoast around Jaffa, and Simeon in the Negev.

The Danites were expelled from their original inheritance by the Amorites and moved on to the sources of the Jordan. Some other tribes also did not succeed in occupying the entire areas assigned to them. Under the monarchy, the men of Simeon seized further land in Seir and the territory of the Amalekites.

The tribal division was maintained under the judges but Solomon adopted a fundamentally different administrative division of the country. After his death, the country split into two. Ten tribes broke off and formed the kingdom of Israel, and the remaining non-Levite tribe, Judah, formed the kingdom of Judah. In 722 B.C.E. the Assyrians conquered the kingdom of Israel, exiling and scattering its inhabitants. Since then, the Ten Tribes' whereabouts has been unknown. Modern Jews as a result are assumed to descend from either the Levites (or a subdivision within them called the *Kohanim* [Jewish priests] or from the tribe of Judah.

TWELVE TRIBES OF ISRAEL IN A NUTSHELL

The nation was divided into twelve tribes during the times of the judges and the early kings. Each tribe of Israel received a portion of land when the Israelites entered Canaan after the Exodus from Egypt. Although each of the tribes was "fathered" by Jacob, they had different "mothers." Leah was the mother of Reuben, Simeon, Levi, Judah, Issachar, and Zebulun. Bilhah (Rachel's maid) was the mother of Dan and Naphtali. Zilpah (Leah's maid) was the mother of Gad and Asher. Finally, Rachel was the mother of Joseph and Benjamin. The tribes slowly lost their distinct identities when Israel became a more consolidated nation.

Following is a summary of the twelve tribes of Israel, their emblems, banners, and jewels:

Name	Emblem	Banner	Jewel
Benjamin	wolf	multicolored	jasper
Dan	serpent	deep blue	jacinth
Naphtali	deer	wine color	amethyst
Asher	woman and olive tree	pearl color	beryl
Levi	urim and tummim	white, red, black	emerald
Judah	lion	sky blue	turquoise
Issachar	donkey	black, sun and moon	sapphire
Zebulun	ship	white	amethyst
Reuben	mandrake	red	carnelian
Simeon	city of Schechem	green	topaz
Gad	encampment	gray	crystal
Ephraim	bullock	jet black	lapis lazuli
Manasseh	unicorn	jet black	lapis lazuli

214

79
VISITING THE SICK

*And the Lord appeared to him (Abraham) by the terebinths
of Mamre, as he sat in the tent door in the heat of the day.*

—Genesis 18:1

DETAILS

The rabbis connected this biblical source verse with Abraham's circumcision and declared that God Himself visited the patriarch during the indisposition that resulted from his circumcision. From this passage they deduced the duty of visiting the sick.

For Jewish people, *bikkur cholim* (Hebrew for "visiting the sick") is one important way of serving one's fellow human being. Visiting the sick is much more than simply a social act that is to be commended. In Judaism, it has the status of a mitzvah, a religious duty, and is counted in the Talmud among the mitzvot to which no limit has been prescribed (Talmud *Shabbat* 127a).

The Bible commands, "And you shall walk in God's ways" (Deuteronomy 28:9). A person is expected to pattern himself or herself upon God's ways. Thus, just as God visited Abraham immediately following his circumcision, so too the Jew has the obligation to visit the sick.

VISITING THE SICK IN A NUTSHELL

According to the Talmud, visiting the sick is one of the precepts for the fulfillment of which a person is rewarded in this world and in the world to come. According to another talmudic statement, whoever visits a sick person helps that person to recover (Nedarim 40a). The purpose of visiting the sick is to cheer them by pleasant conversation and good advice, by rendering them any service and inspiring them with hope.

In many communities today there are special visiting the sick societies, whose function it is to visit those who are in the hospital or confined to the house by illness.

In the anonymous ethical work *Orchot Hayyim* (*Paths of Life*), which has been attributed to Rabbi Eliezer ben Isaac the Great of eleventh-century Germany, we read: "Visit the sick and lighten their suffering. Pray for them and leave. Do not stay long, for you may inflict upon them additional discomfort. And when you visit a sick person, enter the room cheerfully."

80
WAR

When a man takes a wife, he shall be deferred from military duty . . . He shall be free for his house one year and shall cheer his wife whom he has taken.

—Deuteronomy 24:5

When you besiege a city a long time, in making war against it to take it, you shall not destroy the trees thereof by wielding an ax against them. You may eat them, but you shall not cut them down.

—Deuteronomy 20:19

When you draw close to a city to fight against it, then proclaim peace to it.

—Deuteronomy 20:10

DETAILS

Every country has a need for military leadership to protect itself. Certainly Israel and the Jewish people have been involved in their share of wars. Rabbinic thinkers found war quite distasteful, although they certainly realized that there would be times when fighting a war was necessary. It was with this in mind (and based upon biblical battles) that they divided wars into two categories: mandatory wars and those that were optional. Mandatory wars were to be fought for purposes of self-defense, while optional wars were waged to expand territory or to stop an enemy who was about to attack.

WAR IN A NUTSHELL

Ethical rules of warfare developed through the centuries, and the Israelites were bidden to display kindness even in wartime. For instance, in the Bible we learn that a newlywed was exempted from going into battle for a year. Deuteronomy 24:5 states, "when a man takes a wife, he shall be deferred from military duty." The Bible also states (Deuteronomy 20:10) that fruit-bearing trees were not to be destroyed during a siege.

Here are several other biblical and rabbinic statements that help to summarize the Jewish view of war:

- "When a city is laid to siege, it may not be surrounded on all four sides but only on three sides, in order to provide a chance for escape to those who might flee in order to save their own lives" (Maimonides, Code, "Laws of Kings and Wars," 6:7).
- "Rejoice not when your enemy falls in battle, and do not be glad when your enemy is brought down" (Proverbs 24:17).
- "Even on the threshold of war, the Jews are commanded to begin in no other way than with peace, for it is written: 'When you draw near a city to fight, first offer it peace'" (Midrash, Leviticus Rabbah 9).
- "A time for war and a time for peace" (Ecclesiastes 3:8).

81

Water Drawn from the Rock

From the wilderness of Sin the entire Israelite community continued by stages as the Lord would command. They encamped at Rephidim, and there was no water for the people to drink. The people quarrelled with Moses. "Give us water to drink," they said, and Moses replied to them, "Why do you quarrel with me? Why do you try God?" But the people thirsted for water, and the people grumbled against Moses and said, "Why did you bring us up from Egypt, to kill us and our children, and livestock with thirst?" Moses cried out to God, saying, "What shall I do with this people? Before long they will be stoning me." Then the Lord said to Moses, "Pass before the people. Take with you some of the elders of Israel, and take along the rod with which you struck the Nile, and set out. I will be standing there before you on the rock at Horeb. Strike the rock and water will come from it, and the people will drink." And Moses did so in the sight of the elders of Israel.

And God said to Moses: "You and your brother Aaron take the rod and assemble the people, and before their very eyes order the rock to yield its water. Thus shall you produce water for them from the rock and provide drink for the congregation and their beasts."

Moses took the rod from before the Lord, as He had commanded him. Moses and Aaron assembled the congregation in front of the rock, and he said to them, "Listen you rebels, shall we get water for you out of this rock?" And Moses raised his hand and struck the rock twice with his rod. Out came copious water, and the community and their beasts drank. But the Lord said to Moses and Aaron, "Because you did not trust Me enough to affirm My sanctity in the sight of the Israelite people, therefore you shall not lead this congregation into the land that I have given them."

—Numbers 20:7–11

DETAILS

Realizing after they had encamped at Rephidim that there was no water to drink, the Israelites began to quarrel with Moses, asking him to provide them with water. Moses, hearing their complaints, feared for his life and called to God for assistance and divine intervention. In Exodus 16 God spoke to Moses and told him to strike the rock at Horeb. Moses hit the rock and the people were able to drink.

In the later story in the Book of Numbers (chapter 20), Moses was again told that he and Aaron are to take the rod, assemble the community, and order the rock to deliver its water. At the earlier incident Moses had been commanded to physically strike the rock. Here, he was ordered to command the rock verbally to spew forth its water. (No reason was given for the difference in commands.) Instead, Moses struck the rock twice with his rod, and the Israelites were given water. According to this explanation, the miracle was to have rested in the power of the words spoken to the inanimate stone in God's name. Instead, Moses performed a physical act, revealing his lack of trust in God's word. As a result, Moses and Aaron learned that they would not lead the Israelites directly into the Holy Land.

WATER DRAWN FROM THE ROCK IN A NUTSHELL

There are a number of very interesting biblical commentaries related to the two stories of the rock. Maimonides (in his introduction to Ethics of the Father 4), stresses the apparent anger of Moses, who is quoted in the Bible as saying "listen you rebels." The commentator Ibn Ezra thus sees the punishment of Moses as his inability as a leader to control his emotions and anger.

The Alcott Chemin notes that Moses and Aaron said: "Shall **we** get water for you out of this rock?" thereby emphasizing their own rules rather than God's role in the miracle.

To this day modern thinkers find it difficult to understand why Moses' transgression left him with a punishment that does not seem to fit the crime

It is interesting to note that Christian Scriptures have preserved an ancient Jewish legend of a rock containing water that followed the Israelites throughout their trek in the desert (Targum Jonathan on Numbers 21:19). They compare the rock of Meribah to Jesus himself.

82
WORK

Six days a week you shall labor and do all of your work, but the seventh day is the Sabbath of the Lord your God.

—Exodus 20:19

DETAILS

It is a person's God-given duty to work, and Judaism has always stressed the importance of the work ethic and productive work. The Bible itself always exalts work and the worker. God is portrayed in the opening chapters of Genesis as a laborer. In creating the first human, he was told to work the soil. Just as the Torah was given to people as a covenant, so too work was given as a covenant, as it is said: "Six days you shall labor and do all your work, but the seventh day is the Sabbath of the Lord your God" (Exodus 20:9) (Talmud Avot de Rabbi Natan 11).

WORK IN A NUTSHELL

A person who works is able to be self-supporting. The rabbis have taught that in addition to teaching his son Torah, a father must teach his child a trade or a profession (Talmud Kiddushin 29a). Study, the rabbis insisted, cannot be complete when divorced from the world of active work.

Here are some rabbinic statements that sum up the Jewish attitude toward one's God-given task to work:

- "If a person works, that person is blessed" (Midrash Psalm 23:3).
- "Blessing only rests upon the work of a person's hands" (Pesikta Rabbati 19).
- "Greater than a person who fears God is one who eats the fruit of his own labor. Such a person, the Bible says, is twice blessed" (Talmud *Berachot* 8a).
- "How lovely it is when the study of Torah is accompanied by worldly work. It is a safeguard against sin" (Ethics of the Fathers 2:2).
- "If you eat the fruit of the labor of your hands, you will be happy and prosperous" (Psalm 128:2).

83
WRESTLING WITH AN ANGEL

Jacob was left alone. And there wrestled a man with him until the breaking of the day. And when he saw that he was unable to prevail, he touched the hollow of his thigh. And the hollow of his thigh was strained. And he said, "Let me go, for the day breaks." And he said, "I will not let you go, unless you bless me." And he said to him: "What is your name?" And he answered: "Jacob." And he said: "Your name shall no more be called Jacob, but Israel, for you have striven with God and with men, and have prevailed." And Jacob asked, "Tell me I pray, what is your name?" And he answered, "Wherefore is it that you ask after my name?" And he blessed him there. And Jacob called the name of the place Peniel, for "I have seen God face to face, and my life is preserved."

—(Genesis 32:25–31)

DETAILS

As Jacob approached his homeland, the fear of his brother Esau (whom he had not seen in twenty years) revived in him. Jacob knew well that his brother might still wreak vengeance upon him and his family.

As Jacob rose up that night, he first sent his two wives, his two handmaidens, and his eleven children over the Jabbok River, a tributary of the Jordan. Left alone, he wrestled with a "man" until the breaking of the day (Genesis 32:25–31).

Since ancient times, crossing a river has been symbolic of overcoming peril and going forward to a new experience. In this sense, Jacob passing over the Jabbok to meet Esau crossed the watershed of his life. For him to reconcile with his brother Esau, he had to become a different person. His name is changed to Israel meaning "champion of God."

WRESTLING WITH AN ANGEL IN A NUTSHELL

Ancient Near Eastern tradition held that rivers were manifested by demons. Thus, some commentators have argued that the "man" whom Jacob met that fateful night was some type of river demon. The request by the adversary that Jacob let him go before the breaking of dawn serves to fortify the belief that Jacob indeed had encountered a demonic being. For the one who could hold on to a demon long enough could bend him to his will.

Other interpretations of this unknown adversary have emerged. Rabbi Samuel ben Nachman in the Midrash Rabbah (Genesis 38:1) identifies Jacob's adversary as either the angel Michael or Gabriel. These angels are identified in early rabbinic literature as guardian angels who permanently serve God. The Rashbam, a medieval commentator, was of the opinion that since Jacob wished to flee from Esau, God sent the angel from whom he would not flee, so that he might see the fulfillment of God's promise that Esau would do him no harm.

Still other commentators held that Jacob was fighting with his own conscience, eventually emerging from the fight and the dark side of himself, purified in soul and in spirit.

84
BIBLE PORTION SUMMARIES

The first of the Five Books of Moses begins with the creation of the world out of the void. It ends with the last days of Moses. Each week a different *sidrah* (Torah portion) is read on Saturday morning in traditional synagogues. Here is a list of the *Torah* portions for the entire year and a brief summary of their contents.

GENESIS

Contents

The creation of the world. The patriarchs—Abraham, Isaac, and Jacob. Jacob and his sons go down to Egypt. Jacob blesses his sons before his death.

Weekly Portions

Bereshit (1:1–6:8) The world is created in six days.

Noach (6:9–11:32) A flood destroys the world. God's rainbow promises that the world will never again be destroyed in its entirety.

Lekh Lekha (12:1–17:27) Abraham leaves Mesopotamia for the Promised Land.

Vayera (18:1–22:24) Abraham welcomes three angels into his tent and learns that his wife Sarah will give birth to a son.

Chayyei Sarah (23:1–25:18) Eliezer finds a suitable wife, Rebecca, for Abraham's son Isaac.

Toledot (25:19–28:9) The birth of Esau and Jacob. Isaac blesses Jacob.

Vayetze (28:10–32:3) God appears to Jacob in a dream. Jacob works fourteen years and marries Leah and Rachel.

Vayishlach (32:4–36:43) Jacob and Esau reunite after twenty years. Rachel dies and is buried in Bethlehem.

Vayeshev (37:1–40:23) Joseph's brothers strip him of his coat of many colors and throw him into a pit.

Miketz (41:1–44:17) Joseph successfully interprets Pharaoh's dreams. Joseph is appointed viceroy.

Vayigash (44:18–47:27) Joseph reveals himself to his brothers, who are dumbfounded.

Vayechi (47:28–50:26) Jacob blesses his sons. Joseph dies at end of book at age 110.

EXODUS

Contents

The Israelites are enslaved in Egypt. Moses receives the Ten Commandments. The Israelites build a tabernacle.

Weekly Portions

Shemot (1:1–6:1) Moses is saved by Pharaoh's daughter. God appears to Moses at the burning bush.

Va'era (6:2–9:35) God brings plagues upon the Egyptians. Pharaoh's heart hardens and he refuses to let the Israelites go.

Bo (10:1–13:16) Egyptian firstborn children are slain by God. The Israelites hastily leave Egypt and bake matzah from unleavened dough.

Beshallach (13:17–17:16) The waters of the Red Sea divide to make a path for the Israelites.

Yitro (18:1–20:23) Jethro, Moses' father-in-law, advises him to appoint judges so as to ease his burden. Moses receives the Ten Commandments on Mount Sinai.

Mishpatim (21:1–24:18) Moses instructs the Israelites in the Law.

Terumah (25:1–27:19) The tabernacle is constructed.

Tetzaveh (27:20–30:10) Aaron and his sons are put in charge of the menorah. The priestly garments are described in great detail.

Ki Tissa (30:11–34:35) The Israelites build a golden calf; when Moses sees it he shatters the tablets containing the Ten Commandments.

Vayakhel (35:1–38:20) The people bring an array of gifts for the tabernacle until they are told to stop.

Pekudei (38:21–40:38) The cloud of glory covers the completed tabernacle as the Israelites stand in the distance.

LEVITICUS

Contents

The priestly code; the rules pertaining to sacrifices, diet, and morality; and the Land of Israel and festivals are discussed.

Weekly Portions

Vayikra (1:1–5:26) God reveals the sacrificial laws.

Tzav (6:1–8:36) Moses anoints Aaron and his sons as priests.

Shemini (9:1–11:47) Laws describing kosher and nonkosher animals are enumerated.

Tazria (12:1–13:59) Cleanliness and uncleanliness are defined in relation to childbirth and leprosy.

Metzora (13:1–15:33) The laws for the purification of the leper after he has healed are discussed.

Acharei Mot (16:1–18:30) Aaron's sons die. Aaron chooses by lot a goat and a scapegoat.

Kedoshim (19:1–20:27) More laws are set forth, including, "Love your neighbor as yourself."

Emor (21:1–24:23) Festival seasons are described in detail.

Behar (25:1–26:23) The sabbatical and jubilee years are discussed.

Bechukkotai (26:3–27:34) The punishment for rejecting God's covenant is discussed.

NUMBERS

Contents

The Census. More statutes and laws. Adventures of the Hebrews en route to Canaan through the desert.

Weekly Portions

Bamidbar (1:1–4:20) Description of the Israelites' encampments during their journeys through the desert.

Naso (4:21–7:89) Regulations concerning Nazirites and the three-fold priestly benediction.

Behaalotekha (8:1–12:16) Kindling of the *menorah*. Seventy elders are delegated to serve under Moses.

Shelach Lekha (13:1–15:41) Twelve spies are dispatched to survey the land of Canaan. Two of the spies return with a positive report.

Korach (16:1–18:32) Korach refuses to accept the leadership of Moses and Aaron. He and his assembly are killed by an earthquake.

Chukkat (19:1–22:1) The laws regarding the red heifer are enumerated. Moses strikes the rock and water gushes forth.

Balak (22:2–25:9) Balak, king of Moab, sends Bilaam to curse the Israelites. Instead, Bilaam gives his blessing to them.

Pinchas (25:10–30:1) The daughters of Zelophechad are given their father's inheritance. Moses chooses Joshua as his successor.

Mattot (30:2–32:42) Moses informs the tribal heads regarding the laws of vowing.

Masei (33:1–36:13) The detailed account of the various way stations on the Israelites' route to the Promised Land. Reference is made to the cities of refuge.

DEUTERONOMY

Contents

A recapitulation of the laws with some additions. Moses addresses the children of Israel and presents them with some warnings.

Weekly Portions

Devarim (1:1–3:22) Moses explains and interprets the law to the people.

Va'et'chanan (3:23–7:11) The Ten Commandments are repeated, with slight variations. The cities of refuge are mentioned. The first section of the *Shema* is begun with, "You shall love the Lord your God."

Ekev (7:12–11:25) The *Shema* continues with the second paragraph, which deals with the theme of reward and punishment.

Re'eh (11:26–16:17) Moses continues his address, telling the people that obedience will bring them blessing, whereas disobedience will bring them curses.

Shoftim (16:18–21:9) Moses warns the people against idolatry. He also reminds the people of the importance of pursuing justice.

Ki Tetze (21:10–25:19) Moses reviews a variety of laws intended to strengthen family life and human decency in Israel. Those laws refer to lost property, the educational responsibility of parents to their children, and kindness to animals, among other things.

Ki Tavo (26:1–29:8) The laws of tithing and first fruits are discussed.

Nitzavim (29:9–30:20) Moses continues his farewell speech and God tells the people to choose life.

Vayelekh (31:1–30) Joshua is appointed successor to Moses. Moses completes the writing of the Torah.

Haazinu (32:1–52) Moses' farewell song—a beautiful poem in which he calls upon heaven and earth to witness God's dependability.

Vezot HaBerakhah (33:1–34:12) Moses' final blessing poem and the report of Moses' death on Mount Nebo. Israel now turns to Joshua for leadership.

85
Notable Quotations

Every Bible portion of the week has at least one notable quote that has made an indelible mark upon today's society. Following is a listing of the Bible portions of the week and the quotations that have stood the test of time.

BOOK OF GENESIS

Genesis (1–6:8)

1. "And God blessed them saying: Be fruitful and multiply" (Genesis 1:22).
2. "God said: Let us make man in our image, after our likeness" (Genesis 1:26).
3. "God blessed the seventh day and hallowed it, because in it God rested from all the work which God in creating had made" (Genesis 2:3).
4. "Therefore shall a man leave his father and his mother, and

shall cleave to his wife, and they shall be one flesh" (Genesis 2:24).

5. "And the Lord God called to man, and said to him: 'Where are you?'" (Genesis 3:9).

6. "And God said to Cain: 'Where is Abel your brother?' And he said: 'I do not know; am I my brother's keeper?'" (Genesis 4:9).

Noah (Genesis 6:9–11:32)

1. "Noah was in his generations a man righteous and whole-hearted; Noah walked with God" (Genesis 6:9).

2. "Of every living thing of all flesh, two of every sort shall you bring into the ark, to keep them alive with you; they shall be male and female" (Genesis 6:19).

3. "Whosoever sheds man's blood, by man shall his blood be shed; for in the image of God, God made man" (Genesis 9:6).

4. "I have set my bow in the cloud, and it shall be for a token of a covenant between Me and the earth" (Genesis 9:13).

5. "The whole earth was of one language and of one speech" (Genesis 11:1).

6. "They said: 'Come, let us build us a city, and let us make us a name; lest we be scattered abroad upon the face of the whole earth'" (Genesis 11:4).

7. "Therefore the name of it [the city] was Babel, because God confounded there the language of all the earth; and from there did God scatter them abroad upon the face of all the earth" (Genesis 11:9).

Lech Lecha (Genesis 12:1–17:27)

1. "Now God said to Abram: 'Get you out of your country, and from your kindred, and from your father's house, to the land which I will show you'" (Genesis 12:1).
2. "And I will make your seed as the dust of the earth, then shall your seed also be numbered" (Genesis 13:16).
3. "Neither shall your name any more be called Abram, but your name shall be Abraham; for I have made you the father of a multitude of nations" (Genesis 17:5).
4. "You shall be circumcised in the flesh of your foreskin. And it shall be a token of a covenant between Me and you" (Genesis 17:11).

Vayera (Genesis 18:1–22:24)

1. "And the Lord appeared to him [Abraham] by the terebinths of Mamre, as he sat in the tent door in the heat of the day" (Genesis 18:1).
2. "Peradventure there are fifty righteous people within the city. Will You indeed sweep away and not forgive the place for the fifty righteous that are therein?" (Genesis 18:24).
3. "But his [Lot's] wife looked back from behind him, and she became a pillar of salt" (Genesis 19:26).
4. "And God remembered Sarah as God had said, and God did unto Sarah as He had spoken" (Genesis 21:1).
5. "God said: 'Take your son, your only son, whom you love, even Isaac, and go to the land of Moriah; and offer him there for a burnt offering upon one of the mountains of which I will tell you'" (Genesis 22:2).
6. "Abraham said: 'God will provide Himself with the lamb for the burnt offering, my son. So they went both of them together'" (Genesis 22:8).

7. "The angel of God called to him [Abraham] out of heaven and said: 'Abraham, Abraham.' And he said: 'Here am I.'" (Genesis 22:11).

Chaye Sarah (Genesis 23:1–25:18)

1. "[Abraham said] 'I am a stranger and a sojourner with you; give me possession of a burying place with you, that I may bury my dead out of my sight'" (Genesis 23:4).
2. "You [Eliezer, Abraham's servant] shall go to my country, to my kindred, and take a wife for my son, even for Isaac" (Genesis 24:4).
3. "And he [Eliezer] said: 'O God, the God of my master Abraham, send me, I pray You, good speed this day, and show kindness to my master Abraham'" (Genesis 24:12).
4. "Let this come to pass, the damsel to whom I shall say: Let down your pitcher, I pray you, that I may drink; and she shall say: Drink, and I will give your camels drink also; let the same be she that You have appointed for Your servant, even for Isaac" (Genesis 24:14).

Toldot (Genesis 25:19–28:9)

1. "And God said to her [Rebekah]: 'Two nations are in your womb, and two peoples shall be separated from your bowels. And the one people shall be stronger than the other people, and the elder shall serve the younger'" (Genesis 25:23).
2. "Jacob went near to Isaac his father, and he felt him and said: 'The voice is the voice of Jacob, but the hands are the hands of Esau'" (Genesis 27:22).

3. "Behold of the fat places of the earth shall be your (Esau) dwelling, and of the dew of heaven above" (Genesis 27:39).

Vayetze (Genesis 28:10–32:3)

1. "And he (Jacob) dreamed, and behold a ladder set up on the earth, and the top of it reached to heaven. And behold, the angels of God ascending and descending upon it" (Genesis 28:12).
2. "And he (Jacob) was afraid, and he said: 'How awesome is this place. This is none other than the house of God, and this is the gate of heaven'" (Genesis 28:17).

Vayishlach (Genesis 32:4–36:43)

1. "And Jacob was left alone, and there wrestled a man with him until the breaking of the day" (Genesis 32:25).
2. "And he said: 'Your name shall be called no more Jacob, but Israel. For you have striven with God and with men, and have prevailed'" (Genesis 32:29).
3. "And Esau ran to meet him [Jacob], and embraced him, and fell on his neck and kissed him. And they wept" (Genesis 33:4).
4. "And God said to him: 'Your name shall not be called anymore Jacob, but Israel shall be your name'" (Genesis 35:10).

Vayeshev (Genesis 37:1–40:23)

1. "Now Israel loved Joseph more than all his children, because he was the son of his old age, and he made him a coat of many colors" (Genesis 37:3).

2. " . . .'Behold, I [Joseph] have dreamed a dream, and behold, the sun and the moon and the eleven stars bowed down to me'" (Genesis 37:9).

3. "And it came to pass after these things, that his master's wife cast her eyes upon Joseph, and she said: 'Lie with me'" (Genesis 39:7).

4. "Joseph said to them [Pharaoh's officers]: 'Do not interpretations belong to God? Tell it to me, I pray you'" (Genesis 40:8).

Miketz (Genesis 41:1–44:17)

1. "And he slept and dreamed a second time, and behold, seven ears of corn came up upon one stalk, rank and good. And behold, seven ears, thin and blasted with the east wind, sprung up after them. And the thin ears swallowed up the seven rank and full ears" (Genesis 41: 5–7).

2. "And Joseph answered Pharaoh saying: 'It is not in me; God will give Pharaoh an answer of peace'" (Genesis 41:16).

3. "And Pharaoh said to his servants: 'Can we find such a woman as this [Joseph], a man in whom is the spirit of God'" (Genesis 41:38).

Vayigash (Genesis 44:18–47:27)

1. "And we [Joseph's brothers] said to my lord: 'The lad [Benjamin] cannot leave his father. For if he should leave his father, his father would die'" (Genesis 44:22).

2. "And Joseph said to his brothers: 'I am Joseph; does my father yet live?' And his brothers could not answer him, for they were afraid at his presence" (Genesis 45:3).

3. "And God said: 'I am God, the God of your father. Fear not to go down to Egypt, for I will make of you there a great nation'" (Genesis 46:3).

Vayehi (Genesis 47:28–50:26)

1. "Israel beheld Joseph's sons, and said: 'Who are these?' And Joseph said to his father: 'They are my sons, whom God has given me here.' And he said: 'Bring them, I pray you, to me, and I will bless them'" (Genesis 48:8–9).
2. "And he [Jacob] blessed them that day, saying: 'By you shall Israel bless, saying: May God make you like Ephraim and Manasseh.' And he set Ephraim before Manasseh" (Genesis 48:20).
3. "Judah is a lion's whelp. From the prey, my son, have you gone up. He stooped down, he couched as a lion, and as a lioness. Who shall rouse him up?" (Genesis 49:9).
4. "Joseph is a fruitful vine. A fruitful vine by a fountain. Its branches run over the wall" (Genesis 49:22).

BOOK OF EXODUS

Shemot (Exodus 1:1–6:1)

1. "Come, let us deal wisely with them, lest they multiply" (Exodus 1:10).
2. "And he said: 'Who made you a ruler and judge over us? Do you mean to kill us as you [Moses] killed the Egyptians?' And Moses was afraid and said: 'Surely the thing is known'" (Exodus 2:14).
3. "And Moses said: 'I will turn aside now, and see this great sight, why the bush is not burnt'" (Exodus 3:3).

4. "And God said: 'Do not draw near. Take off your shoes from your feet, for the place upon which you stand is holy ground'" (Exodus 3:5).
5. "God said to Moses: 'I am that I am'" (Exodus 3:14).
6. "Pharaoh said: 'Who is this God, that I should hearken to His voice to let Israel go? I know not this God, and moreover, I will not let Israel go'" (Exodus 5:2).

Vaera (Exodus 6:2–9:35)

1. "Moses spoke before God saying: 'Behold, the children of Israel have not listened to me. How then shall Pharaoh hear me, who am of uncircumcised lips?'" (Exodus 6:12).
2. "And God spoke to Moses and Aaron saying: 'When Pharaoh shall speak to you, saying: Show a wonder for you, then you shall say to Aaron: Take your rod, and cast it down before Pharaoh, that it become a serpent'" (Exodus 7:8–9).
3. "Pharaoh's heart was hardened, and he did not listen to them, as God has spoken" (Exodus 7:13).
4. "God said to Moses: 'Say to Aaron: Take your rod and stretch out your hand over the waters of Egypt, over their rivers, over their streams'" (Exodus 7:19).
5. "Then God said to Moses: 'Go into to Pharaoh and tell him: Thus says the Lord, God of the Hebrews: Let My people go, that they may serve Me'" (Exodus 9:1).

Bo (Exodus 10:1–13:16)

1. "Moses and Aaron went to Pharaoh and said to him: 'Thus says God, the God of the Hebrews: How long will

you refuse to humble yourself before Me?'" (Exodus 10:3).

2. "Moses said: 'We will go with our young and with our old, with our sons and with our daughters, with our flocks and with our herds we will go'" (Exodus 10:9).

3. "And there shall be a cry throughout the land of Egypt, such as there has been none like it, nor shall be like it any more'" (Exodus 11:6).

4. "You shall take of the blood, and put it on the two side-posts and on the lintel, upon the houses wherein they shall eat" (Exodus 12:7).

5. "Seven days you shall eat unleavened bread; howbeit the first day you shall put away leaven out of your houses" (Exodus 12:15).

6. "It came to pass at midnight, that God smote all the first born in the land of Egypt, from the first born of Pharaoh that sat on his throne unto the first born of the captive that was in the dungeon; and all the first born of cattle" (Exodus 12:29).

7. "They [the Israelites] baked unleavened cakes of dough which they brought forth out of Egypt, for it was not leavened. Because they were thrust out of Egypt, and could not tarry" (Exodus 12:39).

8. "God spoke to Moses saying: 'Sanctify unto Me all the first born, whatever opens the womb among the children of Israel, both of man and of beast, it is Mine'" (Exodus 13:1–2).

9. "You shall tell your son in that day saying: 'It is because that which God did for me when I came forth out of Egypt'" (Exodus 13:8).

10. "It shall be for a sign unto your hand, and for frontlets between your eyes. For by strength of hand God brought us forth out of Egypt" (Exodus 13:16).

Beshallach (Exodus 13:17–17:16)

1. "And it came to pass, when Pharaoh had let the people go, that God led them not by the way of the land of the Philistines, although that was near. For God said: 'Lest perhaps the people repent when they see war, and they return to Egypt'" (Exodus 13:17).
2. "The pillar of cloud by day, and the pillar of fire by night did not depart from the people" (Exodus 13:22).
3. "God said to Moses: 'Why do you cry to Me? Speak to the children of Israel, that they may go forward'" (Exodus 14:15).
4. "Moses stretched out his hand over the sea, and God caused the sea to go back by a strong east wind all the night, and made the sea dry land, and the waters were divided. And the children of Israel went into the midst of the sea upon dry ground" (Exodus 14:21–22).
5. "The Lord is my strength and my song, and God is become my salvation. This is my God and I will glorify Him. My father's God, and I will exalt Him" (Exodus 15:2).
6. "Who is like unto You, O God, among the mighty? Who is like unto You, glorious in holiness, revered in praises, doing wonders?" (Exodus 15:11).
7. "The children of Israel said to them: 'Would that we had died by the hand of God in the land of Egypt, when we sat by the flesh pots, when we ate bread to the full. For you have brought us forth to this wilderness, to kill this whole assembly by hunger'" (Exodus 16:3).
8. "Behold, I [Moses] will stand before you there upon the rock in Horeb; and you shall smite the rock, and there shall come water out of it, that the people may drink" (Exodus 17:6).
9. "God said to Moses: 'Write this for a memorial in the book, and rehearse it in the ears of Joshua. For I will utterly blot

out the remembrance of Amalek from under heaven'"
(Exodus 17:14).

Yitro (Exodus 18:1–20:23)

1. "You have seen what I did to the Egyptians, and how I bore you on eagles' wings, and brought you unto Myself" (Exodus 19:4).
2. "If you will listen to My voice, and keep My covenant, then you shall be My own treasure from among all peoples. For all the earth is Mine" (Exodus 19:5).
3. "And it came to pass on the third day, when it was morning, that there were thunders and lightnings and a thick cloud upon the mount, and the voice of a horn exceeding loud. And all the people that were in the camp trembled" (Exodus 19:16).
4. "God spoke all these words, saying: 'I am the Lord your God, who brought you out of the land of Egypt, out of the house of bondage'" (Exodus 20:1–2).
5. "Remember the sabbath day to keep it holy" (Exodus 20:8).
6. "Honor your father and your mother, that your days may be long upon the land which the Lord God gives you" (Exodus 20:12).
7. "All the people perceived the thunder and the lightnings, and the voice of the horn, and the mountain smoking, and when they saw it, they stood afar off" (Exodus 20:15).

Mishpatim (Exodus 21:1–24:18)

1. "He that smites a man, so that dies, shall surely be put to death" (Exodus 21:12).

2. "If men strive together, and hurt a woman with child, so that her fruit depart, and yet no harm follow, he shall be surely fined, according as the woman's husband shall lay upon him; and he shall pay as the judges determine. But if any harm follow, then you shall give an eye for an eye, tooth for tooth, hand for hand, foot for foot" (Exodus 21:23–24).

3. "And a stranger you shall not wrong, neither shall you oppress him. For you were strangers in the land of Egypt" (Exodus 22:20).

4. "You shall not wrest the judgment of your poor in his cause" (Exodus 23:6).

5. "You shall not seethe a kid in its mother's milk" (Exodus 23:19).

Terumah (Exodus 25:1–27:19)

1. "And God spoke to Moses saying: 'Speak to the children of Israel, that they take for Me an offering; of every man whose heart makes him willing you shall take My offering'" (Exodus 25:1–2).

2. "And let them make Me [God] a sanctuary, that I may dwell among them" (Exodus 25:8).

Tetzaveh (Exodus 27:20–30:10)

1. "You shall command the children of Israel, that they bring to you pure olive oil, beaten for the light, to cause a lamp to burn continually" (Exodus 27:20).

2. "You shall put on the breastplate of judgment the Urim and the Thummim, and they shall be upon Aaron's heart, when he goes in before the Lord" (Exodus 28:30).

3. "When Aaron lights the lamps at dusk, he shall burn it, a perpetual incense before the God throughout your generations" (Exodus 30:8).

Ki Tissa (Exodus 30:11–34:35)

1. "The rich shall not give more, the poor shall not give less, than the half-shekel, when they give the offering of the Lord, to make atonement for your souls" (Exodus 30:15).
2. "Six days work shall be done, but on the seventh day is a sabbath of solemn rest, holy to God. Whosoever does any work in the sabbath day, that person shall surely be put to death. Wherefore the children of Israel shall keep the sabbath, and observe it throughout their generation as an everlasting covenant" (Exodus 31:15–16).
3. "When the people saw that Moses delayed to come down from the mountain, the people gathered themselves together to Aaron and said to him: 'Make us a god who shall go before us, for as for this Moses, the man that brought us up out of the land of Egypt, we know not what is become of him'" (Exodus 32:1–2).
4. "Moses besought the Lord his God and said: 'God, why does Your anger wax hot against Your people, that You have brought forth out of the land of Egypt with great power and a mighty hand. Wherefore should the Egyptians speak saying: For evil did He bring them forth, to kill them in the mountains, and to consume them from the face of the earth? Turn from Your fierce wrath, and repent of this evil against Your people'" (Exodus 32:11–12).
5. "And it came to pass, as soon as Moses came near to the camp, that he saw the calf and the dancing; and Moses' anger waxed hot, and he cast the tablets out of his hands, and broke them beneath the mount" (Exodus 32:19).

6. "And he [Moses] said: 'Show me I pray Your glory'" (Exodus 33:19).
7. "I [God] will take away My hand, and you shall see My back, but My face shall not be seen" (Exodus 33:23).
8. "And the Lord descended in the cloud, and stood with him there, and proclaimed the name of the Lord. And the Lord passed by before him and proclaimed: 'Lord, the Lord God, merciful and gracious, long suffering and abundant in goodness and truth, keeping mercy to the thousandth generation, forgiving iniquity and transgression and sin; and that will by no means clear the guilty; visiting the iniquity of the fathers upon the children, and upon the children's children, unto the third and the fourth generation'" (Exodus 34:5–7).
9. "Three times in the year shall all your males appear before the Lord God, the God of Israel" (Exodus 34:23).
10. "And it came to pass, when Moses came down from Mount Sinai with the two tablets of the testimony in Moses' hand, when he came down from the mount, that Moses did not know that the skin of his face sent forth beams of light while he talked with him" (Exodus 34:29).

Vayakhel (Exodus 35:1–38:20)

1. "You shall kindle no fire throughout your dwellings upon the sabbath day" (Exodus 35:3).
2. "And God has filled him [Bezalel] with the spirit of God, in wisdom, in understanding and in knowledge, and in all manner of workmanship" (Exodus 35:31).
3. "Moses gave commandment, and they caused it to be proclaimed throughout the camp, saying: 'Let neither man nor woman make any more work for the offering of the sanctuary.' So the people were restrained from bringing.

For the stuff they had was sufficient for all the work to make it, and too much" (Exodus 36:6–7).

Pekudei (Exodus 38:21–40:38)

1. "And God spoke to Moses saying: 'On the first day of the first month shall you rear up the tabernacle of the tent of meeting'" (Exodus 40:1–2).
2. "Then the cloud covered the tent of meeting, and the glory of God filled the tabernacle" (Exodus 40:34).
3. "The cloud of the Lord was upon the tabernacle by day, and there was fire therein by night, in the sight of all the house of Israel, throughout all their journeys" (Exodus 40:35).

BOOK OF LEVITICUS

Vayikra (Leviticus 1:1–5:26)

1. "If the whole congregation of Israel shall err, the thing being hid from the eyes of the assembly, and do any of the things that God has commanded not to be done, and are guilty. When the sin wherein they have sinned is known, then the assembly shall offer a young bullock for a sin offering, and bring it before the tent of meeting" (Leviticus 4:14).
2. "God spoke to Moses saying: 'If any one commit a trespass, and sin by error, then he shall bring his forfeit to God, a ram without blemish out of the flock'" (Leviticus 5:14–15).

Tzav (Leviticus 6:1–8:36)

1. "Fire shall be kept burning upon the altar continually; it shall not go out" (Leviticus 6:6).
2. "At the door of the tent of meeting shall you abide day and night seven days, and keep the charge of the Lord, that you do not die. For so am I commanded" (Leviticus 8:35).

Shemini (Leviticus 9:1–11:47)

1. "Nadav and Avihu, the sons of Aaron, each took of them his censer, and put fire therein, and laid incense thereon, and offered strange fire before the Lord, which He had not commanded them" (Leviticus 10:1).
2. "Then Moses said to Aaron: 'This is it that God has spoken saying: Through them that are near to Me I will be sanctified, and before all the people I will be glorified.' And Aaron held his peace" (Leviticus 10:3).
3. "Whatsoever parts the hoof, and is wholly cloven-footed, and chews the cud, among the beasts, that may you eat" (Leviticus 12:3).
4. "All that do not have fins and scales in the seas, and in the rivers, of all that swarm in the waters, and of all the living creatures that are in the waters, they are a detestable thing to you" (Leviticus 11:10).
5. "For I am the Lord that brought you up out of the land of Egypt to be your God. You shall therefore be holy, for I am holy" (Leviticus 11:45).

Tazria (Leviticus 12:1–13:59)

1. "Speak to the children of Israel saying: 'If a woman be delivered, and bear a male child, then she shall be unclean seven days'" (Leviticus 12:2).
2. "This is the law of the plague of leprosy in a garment of wool or linen, or in the warp, or in the woof, or in any thing of skin, to pronounce it clean, or to pronounce it unclean" (Leviticus 13:59).

Metzora (Leviticus 14:1–15:33)

1. "He [the priest] shall sprinkle upon him that is to be cleansed from the leprosy seven times, and shall pronounce him clean" (Leviticus 14:7).
2. "To teach what is unclean and when it is clean, this is the law of leprosy" (Leviticus 14:57).

Acharei Mot (Leviticus 16:1–18:30)

1. "And Aaron shall cast lots upon the two goats; one goat for the Lord, and the other lot for Azazel" (Leviticus 16:9).
2. "And Aaron shall lay both his hands upon the head of the live goat, and confess over him all the iniquities of the children of Israel, and all their transgressions, even all their sins. And he shall put them upon the head of the goat, and shall send him away by the hand of an appointed man into the wilderness" (Leviticus 16:21).
3. "And it shall be a statute for ever unto you: in the seventh month, on the tenth day of the month, you shall afflict your souls, and shall do no manner of work, the homeborn or the stranger that sojourns among you" (Leviticus 16:29).

4. "Therefore I said to the children of Israel: No soul of you shall eat blood, neither shall any stranger that sojourns among you eat blood" (Leviticus 17:12).

5. "Do not lie with a male as one lies with a woman; it is an abomination" (Leviticus 18:22).

Kedoshim (Leviticus 19:1–20:27)

1. "You shall fear every man his mother and his father, and you shall keep My sabbaths: I am the Lord your God" (Leviticus 19:3).

2. "When you reap the harvest of your land, you shall not totally reap the corner of your field, neither shall you gather the gleaning of your harvest" (Leviticus 19:9).

3. "You shall not oppress your neighbor, nor rob him; the wages of a hired servant shall not abide with you all night until the morning. You shall not curse the deaf, nor put a stumbling block before the blind, but you shall fear your God: I am the Lord" (Leviticus 19:14).

4. "You shall not go up and down as a talebearer among your people. Neither shall you stand idly by the blood of your neighbor: I am the Lord" (Leviticus 19:16).

5. "You shall not take vengeance, nor bear any grudge against the children of your people, but you shall love your neighbor as yourself: I am the Lord" (Leviticus 19:18).

6. "You shall rise up before the elderly, and honor the face of the old man, and you shall fear your God: I am the Lord" (Leviticus 19:32).

Emor (Leviticus 21:1–24:23)

1. "Speak to Aaron and his sons, that they separate themselves from the holy things of the children of Israel, which they

allow unto Me, and that they do not profane My holy name: I am the Lord" (Leviticus 22:2).

2. "On the fifteenth day of the same month is the feast of unleavened bread unto God; seven days you shall eat unleavened bread" (Leviticus 23:6).

3. "You shall count unto you from the morrow after the day of rest, from the day that you brought the sheaf of the waving; seven weeks shall there be complete" (Leviticus 33:15).

4. "In the seventh month, in the first day of the month, shall be a solemn rest for you, a memorial proclaimed with the blast of rams horns, a holy convocation" (Leviticus 33:24).

5. "You shall dwell in booths seven days" (Leviticus 33:42).

6. "You shall have one manner of law, as well for the stranger, as for the homeborn, for I am the Lord your God" (Leviticus 34:22).

Behar (Leviticus 25:1–26:2)

1. "Six years shall you sow your field, and six years you shall prune your vineyard, and gather in the produce thereof. But in the seventh year shall be a sabbath of solemn rest for the land, a sabbath unto God. You shall neither sow your field, nor prune your vineyard" (Leviticus 25:4).

2. "You shall number seven sabbaths of years for you, seven times seven years, and there shall be unto you the days of seven sabbaths of years, even forty and nine years. Then you shall make a proclamation with the blast of the horn on the tenth day of the seventh month . . . And you shall hallow the fiftieth year, and proclaim liberty throughout the land to all the inhabitants thereof; it shall be a jubilee for you, and you shall return every person unto his possession, and

you shall return every man to his family" (Leviticus 25:
8–10).

Bechukkotai (Leviticus 26:3–27:34)

1. "If you walk in My statutes and keep My commandments
   and do them, then I will give your rains in their season, and
   the land shall yield her produce, and the trees of the field
   shall yield their fruit" (Leviticus 26:3).
2. "If you shall reject My statutes, and if your soul abhor My
   ordinances, so that you will not do My commandments,
   but break My covenant. I will do this to you: I will appoint
   terror over you, even consumption and fever, that shall
   make the eyes to fail, and the soul to languish" (Leviticus
   26:14–16).
3. "And all the tithe of the herd or flock, whatever passes
   under the rod, the tenth shall be holy to God" (Leviticus
   27:32).

BOOK OF NUMBERS

Bamidbar (Numbers 1:1–4:20)

1. "From twenty years old and upward, all that are able to go
   forth to war in Israel, you shall number them by their
   houses, even you and Aaron" (Numbers 1:3).
2. "I have taken the Levites from among the children of Israel
   instead of every first born that opens the womb among the
   children of Israel. And the Levites shall be Mine" (Numbers
   3:12).

Naso **(Numbers 4:21–7:89)**

1. "The priest shall cause her [suspected adulteress] to swear, and shall say to the woman: 'If no man has lain with you, and if you have not gone aside to uncleanliness, being under your husband, you shall be free from this water of bitterness that causes the curse'" (Numbers 5:19).
2. "Speak to the children of Israel and say to them: When either man or woman shall clearly utter a vow, the vow of a Nazirite, to consecrate himself to the Lord, he shall abstain from wine and strong drink" (Numbers 6:2–3).
3. "The Lord spoke to Moses saying: 'Speak to Aaron and unto his sons, saying: On this wise you shall bless the children of Israel and you shall say to them: The Lord bless you and keep you; The Lord make His face to shine upon you and be gracious to you; The Lord lift up His countenance upon you and give you peace'" (Numbers 6:22–26).

Behaaolotecha **(Numbers 8:1–12:16)**

1. "And the Lord spoke to Moses saying: 'Speak to Aaron, and say to him: when you light the lamps, the seven lamps shall give light in front of the candlestick'" (Numbers 8:2).
2. "It came to pass, when the ark set forward, that Moses said: 'Rise up, O God, and let Your enemies be scattered; let them that hate You flee before You'" (Numbers 10:35).
3. "We remember the fish which we were wont to eat in Egypt for nought; the cucumbers, the melons, the leeks and the onions and the garlic" (Numbers 11:5).
4. "God said to Moses: 'Gather unto Me seventy men of the elders of Israel, whom you know to be the elders of the people, and officers over them; and bring them to the tent

of meeting, that they may stand there with you'" (Numbers 11:16).

5. "Moses cried to God saying: 'Heal her [Miriam] now, O God, I beseech You'" (Numbers 12:13).

Shelach Lecha (Numbers 13:1–15:41)

1. "God spoke to Moses saying: 'Send men, that they might spy out the land of Canaan, which I give unto the children of Israel'" (Numbers 13:1–2).

2. "And they (Caleb and Joshua ben Nun) told him [Moses] and said: 'We came to the land to which you sent us, and surely it flows with milk and honey'" (Numbers 13:27).

3. "There we saw the Nephilim, the sons of Anak, who come of the Nephilim, and we were in our own sight as grasshoppers, and so we were in their sight" (Numbers 13:33).

4. "God said to Moses: 'How long will this people despise Me, and how long will they not believe in Me, for all the signs which I have brought among them?'" (Numbers 14:11).

5. "God spoke to Moses and Aaron saying: 'How long shall I bear with this evil congregation, that keep murmuring against Me?'" (Numbers 14:26–27).

6. "God spoke to Moses saying: 'Speak to the children of Israel, and bid them that they make fringes in the corners of their garments throughout their generations, and that they put with the fringe of each corner a thread of blue. And it shall be unto you for a fringe, that you may look upon it and remember all the commandments of the Lord, and do them'" (Numbers 15:37–39).

Korach (Numbers 16:1–18:32)

1. "They [Korach and his men] assembled themselves together against Moses and Aaron and said to them: 'You take too much upon you, seeing all the congregation are holy, every one of them, and the Lord is among them; wherefore then you lift yourselves above the assembly of the Lord?'" (Numbers 16:3).

2. "And it came to pass, as he made an end of speaking all these words, that the ground did cleave asunder that was under them. And the earth opened her mouth, and swallowed them up, and their households, and all the men that appertained to Korach, and all their goods" (Numbers 16:31–32).

3. "And it came to pass on the morrow, that Moses went into the tent of testimony, and behold, the rod of Aaron for the house of Levi was budded, and put forth buds, and bloomed blossoms, and bore ripe almonds" (Numbers 17:23).

4. "Everything that opens the womb, of all flesh which they offer unto God, both of man and beast, shall be yours; the firstborn of man shall you surely redeem, and the firstling of unclean beasts shall you redeem. And their redemption money, from a month old, shall you redeem them, shall be according to your valuation, five shekels of silver" (Numbers 18:15–16).

Chukkat (Numbers 19:1–22:1)

1. "This is the statute of the law which God has commanded saying: Speak to the children of Israel, that they bring you a red heifer, faultless, wherein there is no blemish, and upon which never came a yoke" (Numbers 19:2).

2. "He that touches the dead, even any man's dead body, shall be unclean seven days" (Numbers 19:11).

3. "And God spoke to Moses saying: 'Take the rod, and assemble the congregation, you and your brother Aaron, and speak to the rock before their eyes, that it gives forth its water. You shall bring forth to them water out of the rock, so you shall give the congregation and their cattle drink'" (Numbers 20:7–8).

4. "Moses lifted up his hand, and smote the rock with his rod twice. And water came forth abundantly, and the congregation drank, and so did their cattle" (Numbers 20:11).

Balak (Numbers 22:2–25:9)

1. "Come now, I [King of Moab] pray you, curse me this people, for they are too mighty for me" (Numbers 22:6).

2. "God said to Balaam: 'You shall not curse the people, for they are blessed'" (Numbers 22:12).

3. "And the ass saw the angel of the Lord, and she thrust herself unto the wall, and crushed Balaam's foot against the wall, and he smote her again" (Numbers 22:25).

4. "How goodly are Your tents O Jacob, Your dwellings O Israel" (Numbers 24:5).

Pinchas (Numbers 25:10–30:1)

1. "Our father [Zelophehad] died in the wilderness, and he was not among the company of them that gathered themselves together against the Lord in the company of Korach, but he died in his own sin; and he had no sons" (Numbers 27:3).

2. "God spoke to Moses saying: 'The daughters of Zelophe-

had speak right: you shall surely give them a possession of an inheritance among their father's brethren'" (Numbers 27:6–7).

3. "God said to Moses: 'Take Joshua the son of Nun, a man in whom is spirit, and lay your hand upon him'" (Numbers 27:18).

4. "On the eighth day you shall have a solemn assembly; you shall do no manner of servile work" (Numbers 29:35).

Mattot (Numbers 30:2–32:42)

1. "Moses spoke to the heads of the tribes of the children of Israel saying: 'This is the thing which God has commanded. When a man vows a vow to God, or swears an oath to bind his soul with a bond, he shall not break his word; he shall do according to all that proceeds out of his mouth'" (Numbers 30:3).

2. "And God's anger was kindled against Israel, and God made them wander to and fro in the wilderness forty years, until all the generation, that had done evil in the sight of God was consumed" (Numbers 32:13).

Massei (Numbers 33:1–36:13)

1. "These are the stages of the children of Israel, by which they went forth out of the land of Egypt by their hosts under the hand of Moses and Aaron" (Numbers 33:1).

2. "And the cities which you shall give to the Levites, they shall be the six cities of refuge, which you shall give for the manslayer to flee" (Numbers 35:6).

3. "Whoever kills any person, the person shall be slain at the

mouth of witnesses, but one witness shall not testify against any person that he die" (Numbers 35:30).

BOOK OF DEUTERONOMY

Devarim (Deuteronomy 1:1–3:22)

1. "You shall not respect persons in judgment; you shall hear the small and the great alike" (Deuteronomy 1:17).
2. "I commanded Joshua at that time saying: 'Your eyes have seen all that the Lord your God has done to these two kings; so shall the Lord do to all the kingdoms whither you go over'" (Deuteronomy 3:21).

Va'etchanan (Deuteronomy 3:23–7:11)

1. "Get you [Moses] up to the top of Pisgah, and lift up your eyes westward, and northward, and southward, and eastward, and behold with your eyes. For you shall not go over the Jordan" (Deuteronomy 3:27).
2. "You shall not add to the word which I command you, nor shall you diminish from you, that you may keep the commandments of the Lord your God which I commanded you" (Deuteronomy 4:2).
3. "Did ever a people hear the voice of God speaking out in the midst of the fire, as you [Moses] have heard, and lived?" (Deuteronomy 4:33).
4. "You shall love the Lord your God, with all your heart, and with all your soul, and with all your might" (Deuteronomy 6:5).
5. "And you shall write them upon the door posts of your house, and upon your gates" (Deuteronomy 6:9).

6. "God did not set His love upon you, nor choose you, because you were more in number than any people—for you were the fewest of all peoples. But because God loved you, and because God would keep the oath which He swore to your fathers, has God brought you out with a mighty hand, and redeemed you out of the house of bondage, from the hand of Pharaoh king of Egypt" (Deuteronomy 7:7–8).

Ekev (Deuteronomy 7:12–11:25)

1. "All the commandments which I command you this day shall you observe to do, that you may live, and multiply, and go in and possess the land which God swore to your fathers" (Deuteronomy 8:1).
2. "And you shall eat and be satisfied, and bless the Lord your God for the good land which God has given you" (Deuteronomy 8:10).
3. "You say in your heart: My power and the might of my hand has gotten me this wealth" (Deuteronomy 8:17).
4. "Love the stranger, for you were strangers in the land of Egypt" (Deuteronomy 10:19).
5. "And it shall come to pass, if you shall hearken diligently to My commandments which I command you this day, to love the Lord your God and to serve God with all your heart and with all your soul, that I will give the rain of your land in its season, the former rain and the latter rain" (Deuteronomy 11:13–14).

Re'eh (Deuteronomy 11:26–16:17)

1. "Behold, I set before you this day a blessing and a curse. The blessing, if you shall hearken to the commandments of

the Lord your God, which I command you this day. And the curse, if you shall not hearken to the commandments of the Lord your God, but turn aside out of the way which I command you this day, to go after other gods, which you have not known" (Deuteronomy 11:26–27).

2. "Be steadfast in not eating the blood, for the blood is life. And you shall not cat the life with the flesh" (Deuteronomy 12:23).

3. "Every beast that parts the hoof, and has the hoof cloven in two, and chews the cud, among the beasts you may eat" (Deuteronomy 14:6).

4. "You shall surely tithe all the increase of your seed, that which is brought forth in the field year by year" (Deuteronomy 14:22).

5. "At the end of every seven years you shall make a release. And this is the manner of the release; every creditor shall release that which he has lent to his neighbor" (Deuteronomy 15:1–2).

6. "If there be among you a needy man, one of your brothers, within any of your gates, in your land which God has given you, you shall not harden your heart, nor shut your hand from your needy brother. But you shall surely open your hand to him" (Deuteronomy 15:7–8).

7. "Observe the month of Aviv, and keep the Passover unto the Lord your God; for in the month of Aviv the Lord your God brought you forth out of Egypt by night" (Deuteronomy 16:1).

8. "Every man shall give as he is able, according to the blessing of the Lord your God which God has given you" (Deuteronomy 16:17).

Shoftim (Deuteronomy 16:18–21:9)

1. "You shall not wrest judgment, you shall not respect persons. Neither shall you take a gift, for a gift blinds the eyes of the wise, and perverts the words of the righteous" (Deuteronomy 16:19).

2. "Justice, justice shall you pursue, that you may live, and inherit the land which the Lord your God gives you" (Deuteronomy 16:20).

3. "At the mouth of two witnesses, or three witnesses, shall he that is to die be put to death. At the mouth of one witness he shall not be put to death" (Deuteronomy 17:6).

4. "And it shall be, when he [the king] sits upon the throne of his kingdom, that he shall write for himself a copy of this law in a book, out of that which is before the priests the Levites" (Deuteronomy 17:18).

5. "And your eye shall not pity: life for life, eye for eye, tooth for tooth, hand for hand, foot for foot" (Deuteronomy 19:21).

6. " And the officers shall speak to the people, saying: 'What man is there that has built a new house, and has not dedicated it? Let him [newlywed] go and return to his house, lest he die in the battle, and another man dedicate it'" (Deuteronomy 20:5).

7. "When you shall besiege a city a long time, you shall not destroy the trees by wielding an ax against them. You may eat of them, but you shall not cut them down. For is the tree of the field man, that it should be besieged of you?" (Deuteronomy 20:19).

8. "And they [elders of the city] shall speak and say: 'Our hands have not shed this blood, neither has our eyes seen it'" (Deuteronomy 21:7).

Ki Tetze (Deuteronomy 21:10–25:19)

1. "You shall not see your brother's ox or his sheep driven away, and hide yourself from them. You shall surely bring them back to your brother" (Deuteronomy 22:1).
2. "A woman shall not wear that which pertains to a man, neither shall a man put on a woman's garment. Whoever does these things is an abomination to the Lord your God" (Deuteronomy 22:5).
3. "If a bird's nest chance to be before you in the way, in any tree or on the ground, with young ones or eggs, and the dam sitting upon the young, or upon the eggs, you shall not take the dam with the young. You shall let the dam go, but the young you may take for yourself. That it may be well with you, and that you may have length of days" (Deuteronomy 22:6–7).
4. "When you build a new house, then you shall make a parapet for your roof, that you bring not blood upon your house, if any man fall from there" (Deuteronomy 22:8).
5. "You shall not sow your vineyard with two kinds of seed, lest the fullness of the seed which you have sown be forfeited together with the increase of your vineyard" (Deuteronomy 22:9).
6. "You shall not wear a mingled stuff, wool and linen together" (Deuteronomy 22:11).
7. "You shall have a paddle among your weapons, and it shall be, when you sit down abroad, that you shall dig with it, and shall turn back and cover that which comes from you" (Deuteronomy 23:14).
8. "The fathers shall not be put to death for the children, neither shall the children be put to death for the fathers. Every person shall be put to death for his own sin" (Deuteronomy 24:16).

9. "A perfect and just weight shall you have" (Deuteronomy 25:15).
10. "Remember what Amalek did to you by the way as you came forth out of Egypt" (Deuteronomy 25:17).

Ki Tavo (Deuteronomy 26:1–29:8)

1. "You shall take of the first of all the fruit of the ground, which you shall bring in from your land that the Lord God has given you, and you shall place it in a basket, and you shall go to the place which the Lord your God will choose to cause His name to dwell there" (Deuteronomy 26:1).
2. "And you shall speak and say before the Lord your God: 'A wandering Aramean was my father, and he went down to Egypt and sojourned there, few in number. And he became there a nation, great, might and populous'" (Deuteronomy 26:5).
3. "The Egyptians dealt ill with us, and afflicted us, and laid upon us hard bondage" (Deuteronomy 26:6).
4. "Cursed be the one that dishonors his father or his mother. And all the people shall say: Amen" (Deuteronomy 27:16).

Nitzavim (Deuteronomy 29:9–30:20)

1. "You are standing this day all of you before the Lord your God: your heads, your tribes, your elders, and your officers, even all the men of Israel" (Deuteronomy 29:9).
2. "Neither with you only do I [God] make this covenant and this oath. But with him that stands here with us this day before the Lord our God, and also with him that is not here with us this day" (Deuteronomy 29:13–14).
3. "For this commandment which I command you this day, it

is not too hard for you, neither is it far off. It is not in heaven, that you should say: 'Who shall go up for us to heaven, and bring it to us, and make us to hear it, that we may do it?'" (Deuteronomy 30:11–12).

4. "I [God] call heaven and earth to witness against you this day, that I have set before you life and death, the blessing and the curse. Therefore, choose life, that you may live, you and your seed" (Deuteronomy 30:19).

Vayelech (Deuteronomy 31:1–30)

1. Be strong and of good courage, fear not, nor be afraid of them. For the Lord your God, He it is that goes with you. God will not fail you, nor forsake you" (Deuteronomy 31:6).
2. "Moses wrote this law, and delivered it to the priests the sons of Levi, that bore the ark of the covenant of the Lord, and unto all the elders of Israel" (Deuteronomy 31:9).
3. "Now therefore write this song for you, and teach it to the children of Israel. Put it in their mouths, that this son may be a witness for Me against the children of Israel" (Deuteronomy 31:19).

Haazinu (Deuteronomy 32:1–52)

1. "My doctrine shall drop as the rain, My speech shall distill as the dew" (Deuteronomy 32:2).
2. "The Rock, His work is perfect, for all His ways are justice; a God of faithfulness and without sin, just and right is God" (Deuteronomy 32:4).
3. "Remember the days of old, consider the years of many

generations. Ask your father and he will declare to you, your elders and they will tell you" (Deuteronomy 32:7).

4. "And die [Moses] in the mount whither you go up, and be gathered to your people, as Aaron your brother died in mount Hor, and was gathered to his people" (Deuteronomy 32:50).

5. "You [Moses] shall see the land from afar, but you shall not go to the land which I give to the children of Israel" (Deuteronomy 32:52).

Vezot HaBerakhah
(Deuteronomy 33:1–34:12)

1. "Moses commanded us a law, an inheritance of the congregation of Jacob" (Deuteronomy 33:4).

2. "And of Dan he said: Dan is a lion's whelp, that leaps forth from Bashan" (Deuteronomy 33:22).

3. "And he [Moses] was buried in the valley of the land of Moab over against Beth-peor. And no man knows of his grave to this day" (Deuteronomy 34:6).

4. "There has not risen a prophet since in Israel like unto Moses, whom God knew face to face" (Deuteronomy 34:10).

General Index

INDEX OF PASSAGES

About the Author

Rabbi Ronald H. Isaacs has been the spiritual leader of Temple Sholom in Bridgewater, NJ, since 1975. He received his doctorate in instructional technology from Columbia University's Teachers College. He is the author of more than fifty books. His most recent publications include *Every Person's Guide to Death and Dying in the Jewish Tradition* and *Every Person's Guide to Jewish Philosophy and Philosophers*. Rabbi Isaacs currently serves on the publications committee of the Rabbinical Assembly of America and with his wife Leora designs and coordinates the adult learning summer experience called Shabbat Plus at Camp Ramah in the Poconos. He resides in New Jersey with his wife, Leora, and their children, Keren and Zachary.